Profit and Protect: Retail Trading Strategies to Manage Risk and Grow Your Wealth

Foundations to Advanced. Stocks, Bonds, Crypto, Commodities & Forex. Hedging with Options, Swaps, Futures & More

I0416410

By Dr Israel Carlos Lomovasky

About the Book

Unlock Your Trading Potential

In the world of retail trading, where the waves of market volatility constantly challenge the shores of investment, "Profit and Protect: Retail Trading Strategies to Manage Risk and Grow Your Wealth" emerges as the beacon of wisdom for traders seeking to navigate these tumultuous waters with confidence and strategy.

About the Book

"Profit and Protect" is not just another trading book; it's a comprehensive guide that takes you by the hand and walks you through the intricate world of financial markets with the precision of a seasoned trader and the care of a mentor. This book is designed to transform you from a market participant to a market conqueror, focusing on the most critical aspect of trading: Risk Management.

What You Will Learn

- **Fundamental Principles of Trading**: Grasp the basics of the financial markets, understand the different trading instruments, and decode the language of the market.
- **Advanced Risk Management Techniques**: Dive deep into the art and science of risk management with strategies that protect your capital and maximize your profits.
- **Psychological Aspects of Trading**: Conquer the emotional and psychological challenges that stand in the way of trading success.
- **Practical Applications and Real-World Examples**: Bridge the gap between theory and practice with actionable advice, case studies, and real-world examples that bring the concepts to life.
- **Building a Growth-Oriented Portfolio**: Learn how to create and manage a portfolio that not only survives but thrives in the dynamic world of trading.

Who Should Read This Book?

- **Novice Traders**: Embark on your trading journey with a solid foundation and a clear path forward.

- **Seasoned Investors**: Refine your strategies and deepen your understanding of risk management to navigate the markets more effectively.
- **Financial Enthusiasts**: Explore the potential of the financial markets and learn how trading can become a vital part of your investment strategy.

Why "Profit and Protect"?

"Profit and Protect" stands out because it prioritizes the preservation of your capital as the cornerstone of wealth accumulation. Through a meticulous blend of theoretical knowledge and practical insights, this book equips you with the tools and confidence needed to make informed trading decisions.

Take Control of Your Trading Destiny

With "Profit and Protect: Retail Trading Strategies to Manage Risk and Grow Your Wealth," you're not just reading a book; you're stepping into a new era of trading mastery. Embrace the journey towards becoming a proficient and successful trader.

Embark on your path to trading excellence. Profit and Protect your way to financial freedom.

This table of contents for "Profit and Protect: Retail Trading Strategies to Manage Risk and Grow Your Wealth" involves structuring the book in a way that guides the reader from foundational concepts to advanced strategies in risk management and wealth growth through trading. Here's the structure for the book:

Preface

- Introduction to the book's purpose, scope, and who it's for.
- Brief overview of the importance of risk management in retail trading.

Chapter 1: Understanding the Basics of Retail Trading

- Introduction to the financial markets.
- Overview of trading instruments: stocks, bonds, forex, commodities, and cryptocurrencies.
- Understanding market dynamics and trading psychology.

Chapter 2: The Fundamentals of Risk Management

- The concept of risk in trading.
- Types of risks: market, credit, liquidity, operational, and psychological risks.
- The importance of risk management in preserving capital.

Chapter 3: Setting Up for Success

- Creating a trading plan: goals, risk tolerance, strategies.
- Importance of a trading journal to track performance and refine strategies.
- Selecting the right brokerage and trading tools.

Chapter 4: Key Risk Management Techniques

- Position sizing and money management strategies.
- Setting stop-loss orders and take-profit levels.
- Diversification across instruments and asset classes.

Chapter 5: Advanced Risk Management Strategies

- Leveraging options for risk management.
- Understanding and using hedging techniques.
- Risk management in algorithmic trading.

Chapter 6: The Psychological Aspects of Trading

- Emotional biases and how they affect trading decisions.
- Techniques to develop emotional discipline and patience.
- The role of confidence and how to build it responsibly.

Chapter 7: Practical Applications and Strategies

- Real-world examples of risk management in trading.
- Analysis of successful trades and lessons learned.
- Case studies of poor risk management and the lessons from those experiences.

Chapter 8: Building a Growth-Oriented Portfolio

- Strategies for long-term wealth growth through trading.
- Balancing risk and reward in portfolio construction.
- Reassessing and rebalancing the portfolio.

Chapter 9: Staying Informed and Ahead

- The importance of continuous learning and staying informed.
- Resources for retail traders: books, websites, courses, and communities.
- The future of retail trading and emerging trends.

Chapter 10: Creating Your Personal Trading Strategy

- Steps to develop a personalized trading strategy.
- Incorporating risk management into your strategy.
- Testing and refining your approach.

Conclusion

- Summary of key points.
- Encouragement for the journey ahead.
- Final thoughts on the importance of risk management and continuous improvement.

Appendices

- Glossary of trading and risk management terms.
- List of useful trading tools and software.
- Recommended reading and resources for further learning.

This book is designed to take the reader on a journey from the basics of trading to mastering risk management techniques and strategies for wealth growth. Each chapter builds on the previous one, ensuring the reader gains a comprehensive understanding of retail trading and risk management.

DISCLAIMER
The material provided in this book is for informational and educational purposes only and is not intended to be taken as trading or investing advice. The content provided is intended to help you better understand various trading and investing strategies and techniques, but it is not a substitute for professional advice. You should always consult with a licensed financial advisor before making any investment decisions. Additionally, trading and investing in securities involves risk, and you should never invest money that you cannot afford to lose. It is your responsibility to comply with all relevant laws and regulations, including those related to securities trading, in your jurisdiction. By using this book, you agree to hold harmless the author and the publisher from any liability arising out of your use of the information provided.
Any investment decisions made by the user through the use of such content is solely based on the user's independent analysis taking into

consideration your financial circumstances, investment objectives and risk
tolerance found therein unless specifically authorized to do so.
The author is not registered as a securities broker-dealer or an investment
adviser either with the U.S. Securities and Exchange Commission (the
"SEC") or with any state or overseas securities regulatory
authority.The Author is not licensed to provide investment advice.

About the author

Curriculum Vitae

Education:

- Doctor of Science (DSc) in Project Evaluation, Technion, Haifa, Israel
- Master of Science (MSc) in Operations Research, London School of Economics
- Bachelor of Science (BSc) in Industrial and Management Engineering, Technion, Haifa, Israel

Teaching and Academic Research Positions Held:

- Micro Economics
- Macro Economics
- Econometrics
- Statistics
- Mathematics
- Public Finance
- Urban Planning Mathematical Models
- Transportation Science

Urban and Regional Planning Experience:

- Comprehensive Urban Renewal Project Manager (Physical and Social Project) of the East Acco Government Project. Received the title Yakir Acco from the Acco municipality.

Mathematical Modelling Projects:

- Optimal production mix model using linear programming for the Israeli Paper Mill, Hedera.
- Optimal loading and unloading of ships in Ashdod port using mathematical simulation and integer programming models for the Phosphates at the Negev company.
- Optimal mining order for the Phosphates at the Negev company using mathematical linear, integer, and nonlinear programming.
- Optimal ship operation to transport crude oil using a simulation model for the Institute of By Sea Transport at Haifa.
- Traffic assignment mathematical model for the Transportation Science Institute, Technion, Haifa.
- Industrial Land use analysis in the city of Tel Aviv using Principal Factors Analysis for Tel Aviv Municipality.
- Pupils distribution among the Tel Aviv school system using an integer programming model for the Municipality of Tel Aviv.
- Various mathematical programming models for El Al, The Electric Company, Teva, etc., in association with the Representative of SAS in Israel (Maia Computers).
- Truck fleet routing model based on mathematical programming and heuristics models for international clientele.

- Optimal Locomotive and personnel assignment (run cutting problem) to trains using integer programming models for the New York City Transit Authority.
- Statistical analysis for sales for the American Cyanamid company in Pearl River, New Jersey.
- Sales analysis models (econometric and statistical models) for JC Penny, USA.

Professional Experience:

- Founding partner (2006-2011) in the company "Kaul and Lomovasky Holdings Inc" specializing in the computerization of trading using artificial intelligence.
- Internet and Artificial Intelligence Programmer, Developer, and Consultant (2012-2018).
- Developed an AI-based system to calculate the price of apartments in 300 towns in Israel, using VBA Excel Neural Networks (artificial intelligence) pre-processing and presented the prices on a Python Django-based website.
- Author of several books on topics such as algorithmic trading, quantum computing, crypto trading, artificial intelligence, and startup ideas.

Computer Programming Skills:

- C, VBA under Excel, Microsoft Office, HTML, PHP, MATLAB, SAS, Python, Django, Keras, Panda, Cloud AI Applications, TensorFlow, Google Cloud Platform, OpenCV, Adversarial GANs, Computer Vision, Image Classification, Object Recognition, Pose Recognition.
- Quantum computing and quantum machine learning.
- Algorithm development, end-to-end ownership.

Publications:

- List of books published from 2018 to 2023 covering topics such as algorithmic trading, quantum computing, artificial intelligence, futurology, and startup ideas.

-The Future Game: Unleashing AI and Quantum Computing Power in Game Theory.: Beginners to Advanced.Python Code.Case studies:Economics,Finance,Politics,Environment,Social Science,Psychology,Health,More Kindle Edition
By Dr Israel Carlos Lomovasky (Author) Format: Kindle Edition

-AI and Quantum Strategies: Python's Role in Economic Innovation: Foundations to Advanced. With python and Quantum Code in a Computational Economics Range of Case Studies Kindle Edition
by Dr Israel Carlos Lomovasky (Author) Format: Kindle Edition

-Quantum Computing in Finance: Bridging Theory and Practice with Python: Case Studies: Algorithmic Trading, Risk Management, Fraud Detection, Options Pricing ,Economic Forecasting and more
by Dr Israel Carlos Lomovasky (Author)

Book 6 of 6: FINANCE

-Artificial Gods: The Onset of Superior Machine Intelligence and Consciousness: : The Why and How of a Ban on Research Leading To Superintelligence And AI Consciousness Kindle Edition
by Dr Israel Carlos Lomovasky (Author)

-Quantum and Consciousness: Exploring the Mind-Computer Interface: Unveiling the Quantum Mind: Quantum Computing and the Fabric of Consciousness Kindle Edition
by Dr Israel Carlos Lomovasky (Author)

-Quantum Democracy: Unleashing MOTMSDD with Quantum Computing: MOTMSDD : Metaverse Of The Minds Social Direct Democracy (The future implications of the ... and Brain Computer Interface Book 6) Kindle Edition
by Dr Israel Carlos Lomovasky (Author)

-MOTMSDD: Metaverse Of The Minds Social Direct Democracy: Governance and Public Decision Making in The Era of Brain Computer Interface, AI and Metaverse, ... and Brain Computer Interface Book 5) Kindle Edition
by Dr Israel Carlos Lomovasky (Author)

-MOTMSDD Urbanism:Redefining Cities through AI and Metaverse of the Minds Social Direct Democracy: Sustainable Urbanism in the Age of Brain-Computer Interface.Solving Conflicts between Citizen's Needs Kindle Edition
by Dr Israel Carlos Lomovasky (Author)

-AI in Financial Markets: A Guide to Algorithmic Trading with ChatGPT: Python Code. CHATGPT Assistance. Basics to Advanced. Traditional and AI/ML Trading. (FINANCE Book 6) Kindle Edition
by Dr Israel Carlos Lomovasky (Author)

-Python for Financial Freedom: Algorithmic Strategies for Personal Wealth: Trading and Investing. Foundations to Advanced. AI/ML, Risk ,Tax ,and Money Management. Stocks & Crypto (FINANCE Book 5) Kindle Edition
by Dr Israel Carlos Lomovasky (Author)

-Quantum Foundations of Computer Vision: A Guide for Researchers and Practitioners: Python and Quantum Language Code. Future Proof Computer Vision (Quantum Computing Book 3) Kindle Edition
by Dr Israel Carlos Lomovasky (Author)

-MOTMSDD ECONOMICS: From Classical Economics, to Metaverse Of The Minds Social Direct Democracy Economics.: For The Next WELFARE ECONOMICS: Harnessing BCI ... the Metaverse . (FUTURE ECONOMICS Book 1) Kindle Edition
by Dr Israel Carlos Lomovasky (Author)

-Quantum Hedge: Unlocking the Future of Algorithmic Trading. : Python and Quantum Languages Code. Basics to Advanced. Stocks, Forex and Crypto. Theory and Hands on Practice. Kindle Edition
by Dr Israel Carlos Lomovasky (Author)

-Quantum Economics: Rethinking Macro and Micro in the Age of Quantum Computing: Theory and Practice: Python and Quantum Language Code Explained Step by Step (FUTURE ECONOMICS Book 2) Kindle Edition
by Dr Israel Carlos Lomovasky (Author)

-Driving with the Mind: Exploring MOTMSDD and Its Impact on Smart Cities and Autonomous Mobility: MOTMSDD: Metaverse of The Minds Social Direct Democracy: ... Meets The Metaverse (URBANISM Book 4) Kindle Edition
by Dr Israel Carlos Lomovasky (Author)

-AI in Fundamental Analysis: Uncovering Hidden Algorithmic Investment Opportunities with Python.: Machine,Reinforcement and Deep Learning.Complete AI-Driven ... Advanced.Risk Management. (FINANCE Book 2) Kindle Edition
by Dr Israel Carlos Lomovasky (Author)

-Python for AI and Creativity: Unleashing the Power of Artificial Intelligence in the Arts: Basics to Advanced.Visual Arts,Design,Music,Poetry,Storytelling, ... learning-Python Book 3) Kindle Edition
by Dr Israel Carlos Lomovasky (Author)

-Python for Machine Learning. From Intermediate to Advanced Guide With Code.: Unleash the Potential of Advanced Machine Learning in Python. Covering Many ... learning-Python Book 2) Kindle Edition
by Dr Israel Carlos Lomovasky (Author)

-Python for Smart Cities: Machine Learning and Artificial Intelligence Applications for Urban Planning and Infrastructure: Python in Action: ML/AI for Smart ... Infrastructure Management (URBANISM Book 2) Kindle Edition
by Dr Israel Carlos Lomovasky (Author)

-Python for Machine Learning: A Beginner's Guide.From Scratch to intermediate.: Basis For Algorithmic Finance, Trading, Healthcare, Industry, Transportation, ... learning-Python Book 1) Kindle Edition
by Dr Israel Carlos Lomovasky (Author)

-SINGULARITY'S VEIL: THE RISE AND FALL OF HUMANITY. : A TALE BETWEEN SCIENCE FICTION AND FUTUROLOGY. STOP ARTIFICIAL GENERAL INTELLIGENCE NOW. (Future sciences - Futurology - Science fiction Book 6) Kindle Edition
by Dr Israel Carlos Lomovasky (Author)

-KILLING THE BEAST. THE THREAT OF ADVANCING ARTIFICIAL GENERAL INTELLIGENCE.: A CALL TO BAN AGI.SURVIVAL OF HUMANITY ON THE LINE. A CONTRARIAN NARRATIVE ... - Futurology - Science fiction Book 5) Kindle Edition
by Dr Israel Carlos Lomovasky (Author)

-Day Trading Basics to Advanced:A Comprehensive Guide.From Scalping to AI/ML.Algorithmic Trading.Python Code.: Day Trading Decoded:Unlocking Secrets to Profitable Trading.Stocks,Crypto,Options,Forex Kindle Edition
by Dr Israel Carlos Lomovasky (Author)

-BEGINNER'S MACHINE LEARNING AND ARTIFICIAL INTELLIGENCE IN PYTHON FOR FINANCE: A GUIDE.: EXPLORING THE INTERSECTION OF FINANCE AND ML/AI: A PYTHON PRIMER Kindle Edition
by Dr Israel Carlos Lomovasky (Author)

-The Internet Of Minds (IOM). An Essay: The Future Implications of Brain Computer Interface
by Dr Israel Carlos Lomovasky (Author)

-CRYPTO TRADING TECHNICAL ANALYSIS: Apply the technical analysis indicators, time-frames and approaches that fit Crypto Currencies trading characteristics. Kindle Edition
by Dr Israel Carlos Lomovasky (Author)

-QUANTUM MACHINE LEARNING: A COMPREHENSIVE GUIDE WITH PRACTICAL EXAMPLES AND QUANTUM LANGUAGE IMPLEMENTATION: FROM BASICS TO ADVANCED.INCLUDES PYTHON CODE. (Quantum Computing Book 2) Kindle Edition
by Dr Israel Carlos Lomovasky (Author)

-CRYPTO BASICS TO ADVANCED. MAKE MONEY WITH CRYPTO.THE CRYPTO BUSINESS STARTUP BIBLE.: Investing ,trading and beyond. 20 Cryptocurrency profitable strategies. Over 100 startup ideas. Kindle Edition
by Dr Israel Carlos Lomovasky (Author)

-QUANTUM COMPUTING AND OPERATIONS RESEARCH.AN ESSAY.WHAT IS QC AND WHY IT MATTERS TO OR PRACTITIONERS.: THE FUTURE IMPLICATIONS OF QUANTUM COMPUTING ON OPTIMIZATION AND OPERATIONS RESEARCH. Kindle Edition
by Dr Israel Carlos Lomovasky (Author)

-ALGORITHMIC TRADING FROM SCRATCH TO AI/ML STRATEGIES IMPLEMENTED IN PYTHON.FOR CRYPTO,STOCKS,FOREX AND MORE.: RETAIL TRADING SYSTEMS FROM BASIC TO SOPHISTICATED STEP BY STEP. PYTHON FOR YOUR PROJECTS. Paperback – May 17, 2023
by Dr Israel Carlos Lomovasky (Author)

-CRYPTO SENTIMENT ALGO TRADING.PYTHON AND PSEUDO-CODE.: Algo Cryptocurrencies Trade: day, trend, news, swing, arbitrage, bots, contrarian, volume, event, seasonal ,and more strategies. Kindle Edition
by Dr Israel Carlos Lomovasky (Author)

-ALGORITHMIC TRADING STRATEGIES AND TECHNIQUES IN PYTHON, PSEUDO-CODE AND TRADESTATION CODE.: Get your projects started.20 most used techniques and strategies covering all tradeable assets. Kindle Edition
by Dr Israel Carlos Lomovasky (Author)
-ALGORITHMIC TRADING STRATEGIES AND TECHNIQUES IN PYTHON, PSEUDO-CODE AND TRADESTATION CODE.: Get your projects started.20 most used techniques and strategies covering all tradeable assets. Kindle Edition
by Dr Israel Carlos Lomovasky (Author)

-

Preface

Section 1: Introduction to the Book's Purpose, Scope, and Audience

Welcome to "Profit and Protect: Retail Trading Strategies to Manage Risk and Grow Your Wealth." This comprehensive guide is meticulously crafted for individuals venturing into or navigating through the intricate world of retail trading. Our mission transcends mere introduction to trading concepts; we aim to unravel the complexities of risk management and arm you with actionable, effective strategies designed to shield your investments and foster growth.

The journey into trading can be as daunting as it is exhilarating. With an abundance of information and a myriad of strategies available, the path to becoming a successful trader often seems obscured. This book serves as your beacon, illuminating the path with clear, concise guidance, whether you're taking your first steps into trading, seeking to refine your existing strategies, or exploring new opportunities within the financial markets.

Our Audience: "Profit and Protect" is crafted with a diverse readership in mind:

- **The Novice Trader:** Embarking on your trading journey can feel overwhelming. This book lays a solid foundation, introducing you to the fundamental principles of trading, from understanding market dynamics to recognizing potential risks and rewards.
- **The Seasoned Investor:** For those with trading experience, this guide offers a deep dive into advanced risk management techniques. It's designed to refine your strategies, helping you navigate the markets more effectively and with greater confidence.

- **The Curious Explorer:** If you're drawn to the financial markets out of interest or seeking alternative investment avenues, this book provides a comprehensive overview, offering insights into how trading can fit into your broader financial strategy.

The Scope of This Book spans a wide array of topics essential for every trader:

- **Fundamental Principles:** We start with the basics—market mechanics, trading instruments, and the importance of economic indicators. This foundation is crucial for understanding how the markets operate and how to begin trading.
- **Risk Management Techniques:** At the heart of successful trading is effective risk management. We delve into strategies to protect your capital, including position sizing, stop-loss orders, and diversification. These techniques are vital for minimizing losses and maximizing potential gains.
- **Advanced Strategies:** For the experienced trader, we explore advanced topics such as leveraging options for risk management, understanding and using hedging techniques, and the intricacies of algorithmic trading. These concepts are designed to enhance your trading strategy and provide a competitive edge in the markets.
- **Psychological Aspects:** Trading is not just about strategies and numbers; it's also a mental game. We address the psychological challenges traders face, offering advice on how to maintain discipline, manage emotional biases, and build confidence.
- **Practical Applications:** Through real-world examples, case studies, and actionable advice, we bridge the gap

between theoretical knowledge and practical application, enabling you to apply what you've learned directly to your trading activities.

"Profit and Protect" is more than just a book; it's a comprehensive guide designed to accompany you on your trading journey, equipping you with the knowledge, strategies, and confidence needed to navigate the markets successfully. Our goal is to not only educate but also inspire you to achieve your trading objectives, manage risks effectively, and ultimately, grow your wealth through informed and strategic trading decisions. Welcome aboard this exciting journey towards becoming a proficient and successful trader.

Section 2: The Importance of Risk Management in Retail Trading

Risk management is not just a component of trading; it is the very essence that can determine a trader's longevity and success in the financial markets. The journey of trading is fraught with volatility and uncertainty, making risk management an indispensable skill for anyone looking to not just survive but thrive in this environment.

Why Risk Management Matters: At its core, risk management is about making informed decisions to minimize potential losses while maximizing opportunities for gain. It's a delicate balance, requiring a deep understanding of market forces, personal discipline, and, most importantly, a well-thought-out strategy. Without it, traders expose themselves to the whims of market volatility, which can erode capital and undermine confidence.

Protecting Your Capital: The primary goal of risk management is capital preservation. Your trading capital is your lifeline; once depleted, your ability to trade—and thereby generate profits—is severely compromised. Effective risk management strategies ensure that losses are kept to a minimum, safeguarding your capital against the unexpected turns of the market.

- **Example**: Consider the practice of setting stop-loss orders. By determining a maximum loss threshold for each trade, you effectively put a safety net under your investment, ensuring that a sudden market downturn doesn't lead to catastrophic losses.

Enhancing Trading Performance: Beyond capital preservation, good risk management enhances your overall trading performance. By carefully selecting your trades, sizing your positions appropriately, and setting realistic profit targets, you can improve your win-rate and profitability over time.

- **Real-World Example**: A trader who diversifies their portfolio across different asset classes (stocks, forex, commodities) can mitigate the impact of a poor performance in any single market. This diversification, a fundamental risk management technique, helps stabilize returns even in turbulent market conditions.

Contributing to Long-Term Wealth Accumulation: The ultimate goal of trading is not just to make profits but to grow wealth sustainably over the long term. Sound risk management is pivotal in this endeavor. By consistently applying risk management principles, traders can compound their gains, turning modest profits into significant wealth over time.

- **Insight**: One of the key strategies for long-term wealth accumulation is the reinvestment of profits into well-researched, diversified assets. By managing risks and carefully reinvesting, traders can benefit from the power of compounding, significantly increasing their investment portfolio's value over the years.

Exploring Dimensions of Risk: Retail trading encompasses various risks, including market risk, liquidity risk, and psychological risk. Understanding these different aspects is crucial for developing an effective risk management strategy.

- **Expert Insight**: Market risk, or the possibility of losses due to market fluctuations, can be mitigated through diversification and the use of hedging instruments. Liquidity risk, the risk that an asset cannot be quickly sold at an expected price, requires careful market selection and timing. Psychological risks, such as the tendency to let emotions guide trading decisions, can be managed through discipline and a strict adherence to pre-defined trading plans.

Conclusion

The emphasis on risk management throughout this book is intentional and critical. It is the framework within which successful trading strategies are built and executed. As we delve deeper into the specifics of trading instruments, market analysis, and advanced trading techniques in the subsequent chapters, the underlying theme of risk management will remain a constant guide. Our aim is to equip you with the knowledge and tools necessary not only to navigate the markets with confidence but to do so in a way that prioritizes the preservation and growth of your capital. Welcome to a journey where risk management is not just a practice but a principle for trading success.

.

Chapter 1: Understanding the Basics of Retail Trading

Section 1.1 Introduction to the Financial Markets

The financial markets are the backbone of the global economy, acting as a platform for buyers and sellers to exchange financial assets. These markets include stock exchanges like the New York Stock Exchange (NYSE) and the NASDAQ, which are pivotal in determining the economic direction through the trading of stocks, bonds, and commodities.

Understanding Market Dynamics:

- **Market Liquidity:** Refers to the ease with which assets can be bought or sold in the market without affecting their price. High liquidity is associated with a high volume of activity.
- **Volatility:** This measures the degree of variation in the price of a financial instrument over time. Markets can experience high volatility, which can present both opportunities and risks for traders.
- **Economic Indicators:** These are statistical metrics used to gauge the health of the economy. They can include employment rates, GDP growth, and inflation. Economic indicators have a profound impact on market movements.
- **Geopolitical Events:** Events such as elections, wars, and trade agreements can significantly affect market sentiment and, consequently, market dynamics.
- **Market Sentiment:** This is the overall attitude of investors toward a particular market or financial asset. Sentiment can be influenced by news, reports, and global events, driving market trends.

In this Chapter, we'll delve deeper into how these elements interact within the global financial markets, influencing trading strategies and investment decisions. By understanding these basics, traders can better navigate the complexities of the markets, setting a solid foundation for risk management and wealth growth strategies.

This introduction aims to set the stage for a comprehensive exploration of retail trading, emphasizing the importance of a strong foundational knowledge in financial markets for successful trading and risk management.

SSection 1.2 Overview of Trading Instruments

In the realm of retail trading, investors have a vast selection of instruments at their disposal, each offering unique opportunities and risks. Understanding these instruments is crucial for developing a diversified investment strategy that aligns with your financial goals and risk tolerance. Let's delve into the main categories:

Stocks
Stocks represent shares of ownership in a company, making shareholders partial owners of that company. The value of stocks fluctuates based on several factors:

- **Company Performance**: Earnings reports, new product launches, and other corporate actions can significantly impact stock prices. For example, a positive earnings report might boost investor confidence, leading to a price increase.
- **Economic Factors**: Changes in interest rates, inflation, and economic growth forecasts can affect the entire stock market. For instance, rising interest rates often lead to lower stock prices as investors seek higher yields elsewhere.
- **News and Events**: News events, both related and unrelated to the company's direct operations, can influence stock prices. An oil company's stock, for example, might rise on news of an oil shortage.

Stocks are a cornerstone of most investment portfolios due to their potential for high returns, but they also carry a significant risk of loss.

Bonds

Bonds are debt instruments issued by corporations and governments to raise capital. When you buy a bond, you're lending money to the issuer in exchange for regular interest payments and the return of the bond's face value at maturity. Key concepts include:

- **Yield**: The annual return on the bond, which can be fixed or variable. Higher yields typically indicate higher risk.
- **Maturity**: The time at which the bond will be repaid. Bonds can range from short-term (a few years) to long-term (several decades).
- **Interest Rate Risk**: The inverse relationship between bond prices and interest rates means that as interest rates rise, bond prices tend to fall, and vice versa.

Bonds are generally considered safer than stocks but offer lower potential returns.

Forex (Foreign Exchange Market)

The forex market is where currencies are traded, making it the largest financial market globally. Factors affecting currency values include:

- **Economic Indicators**: Data such as GDP growth, employment rates, and inflation impact currency strength.

- **Interest Rates**: Higher interest rates offer lenders higher returns relative to other countries, increasing demand for that currency.
- **Geopolitical Stability**: Countries perceived as politically stable attract more foreign investment, strengthening their currency.

Forex trading is complex and involves significant risk, including leverage that can amplify losses.

Commodities

Commodities are basic goods used in commerce that are interchangeable with other goods of the same type, including metals like gold and silver, energy products like oil and natural gas, and agricultural products like wheat and cotton. Prices are influenced by:

- **Supply and Demand**: Shortages or surpluses can cause sharp price movements.
- **Geopolitical Issues**: Political instability in critical supply regions can disrupt supply and increase prices.
- **Seasonal Cycles**: Agricultural commodities, in particular, are subject to seasonal changes that affect supply and prices.

Commodities trading can be a way to hedge against inflation and diversify a portfolio.

Cryptocurrencies

Cryptocurrencies are digital or virtual currencies secured by cryptography, with Bitcoin and Ethereum being the most well-known. They are characterized by their decentralization and often volatility. Influencing factors include:

- **Market Sentiment**: Investor enthusiasm can drive rapid price increases, while negative news can lead to sharp declines.
- **Regulatory News**: Announcements of government regulation can have significant impacts on prices.
- **Adoption and Use Cases**: Increased adoption by businesses and consumers can drive demand and price.

Cryptocurrency investments are highly speculative and subject to both high risk and high reward.

By understanding these trading instruments, retail traders can make informed decisions about where to allocate their investments to align with their financial goals, risk tolerance, and market outlook.

Section 1.3 Understanding Market Dynamics

Market dynamics are critical elements that directly influence trading decisions and financial market movements. By understanding these dynamics, traders can better navigate the complexities of the market and make more informed decisions. Let's dive into the key aspects of market dynamics.

Supply and Demand
The foundational concept of supply and demand is at the heart of market dynamics. It dictates that the price of an asset is directly influenced by the quantity of the asset available (supply) and the desire of buyers to own it (demand).

- **Example**: If a new technology company launches an innovative product that attracts significant interest, the demand for the company's stock may increase. If the supply of shares remains constant or decreases, the stock price is likely to rise.

Market Trends

Market trends refer to the general direction in which the market or an asset's price is moving, categorized into bullish or bearish markets.

- **Bullish Market**: Characterized by rising prices and optimism among investors. A continuous increase in the stock market index over a period is a classic sign of a bullish market.
- **Bearish Market**: Defined by falling prices and a general sense of pessimism. If a market index shows a persistent decline, it's considered to be in a bearish phase.

Understanding these trends helps traders align their strategies with the market's direction.

Economic Data Releases

Economic indicators such as GDP growth rates, unemployment figures, and inflation rates have a profound impact on market sentiment and asset prices.

- **Example**: A higher than expected inflation rate might lead to a decrease in bond prices, as inflation erodes the real value of future fixed payments from bonds.

News and External Factors

News and external factors including political events, natural disasters, or significant policy changes by central banks can cause sudden and significant market fluctuations.

- **Example**: An unexpected political event that increases instability in a region could lead to a decrease in the value of assets associated with that region as investors seek safer investments.

Interpreting Market Dynamics

Traders interpret these dynamics through various means, including technical analysis, fundamental analysis, and sentiment analysis. Technical analysis involves studying price charts to identify patterns and trends. Fundamental analysis looks at economic indicators and company financials to assess an asset's true value. Sentiment analysis gauges the mood of the market to predict future movements based on current feelings.

- **Technical Analysis Example**: A trader might use moving averages to identify a potential bullish reversal in a previously bearish stock.
- **Fundamental Analysis Example**: Evaluating a company's earnings reports to decide if the stock is undervalued or overvalued.
- **Sentiment Analysis Example**: Monitoring social media and news to gauge investor sentiment towards a particular asset.

By understanding and applying insights from market dynamics, traders can better anticipate market movements and adjust their strategies accordingly, aiming to protect their investments and capitalize on opportunities for growth.

Section 1.4 Trading Psychology

Trading psychology plays a pivotal role in the decision-making processes of traders, influencing actions and outcomes in the financial markets. Understanding and managing one's emotional responses is crucial for success in trading.

Emotional and Psychological Challenges
Fear and Greed: These are two primary emotions that traders must contend with. Fear can cause traders to sell their positions too early or prevent them from taking necessary risks, leading to missed opportunities. Conversely, greed can lead to holding onto positions for too long in the hope of higher profits, risking significant losses.

Herd Mentality: This refers to the tendency of traders to follow the majority, often leading to irrational market bubbles or crashes. Individual analysis and judgment are overshadowed by the fear of missing out (FOMO), pushing traders to make decisions based on collective behaviour rather than sound strategy.

Developing a Disciplined Trading Mindset
Emotional Control: Traders need to cultivate emotional resilience, allowing them to stay calm and rational during market volatility. Techniques such as meditation, regular breaks, and setting strict trading hours can help maintain emotional equilibrium.

Patience: Success in trading often requires a long-term perspective and the patience to wait for the right trading opportunities. Developing patience involves setting realistic goals, understanding market cycles, and acknowledging that not all trades will be profitable.

Objectivity: Maintaining objectivity is essential to assess situations accurately and make informed decisions. Traders should rely on comprehensive market analysis and avoid making impulsive decisions based on transient emotions.

Strategies for a Disciplined Trading Approach

1. **Pre-Trade Preparation**: Before entering a trade, define your strategy, including entry and exit points, and adhere to it. This preparation helps mitigate emotional decision-making in the heat of the moment.
2. **Journaling**: Keeping a trading journal is an effective way to reflect on both successful and unsuccessful trades. Documenting the reasoning behind each trade and its outcome helps identify emotional triggers and patterns in decision-making.
3. **Continuous Learning**: Engaging in regular education about markets and trading strategies strengthens confidence and reduces the likelihood of emotional trading. Knowledge is a powerful tool against fear and greed.
4. **Risk Management**: Implementing solid risk management strategies, such as setting stop-loss orders, helps protect against significant losses, reducing the emotional stress associated with trading.
5. **Seeking Support**: Joining trading communities or seeking mentorship can provide emotional support and guidance. Sharing experiences with fellow traders can offer new perspectives and reduce feelings of isolation.

By addressing the psychological aspects of trading head-on, traders can develop the mental fortitude required to navigate the complexities of the markets. A disciplined mindset, combined with effective emotional management strategies, lays the foundation for a successful trading career.

By the end of this chapter, readers will have a solid foundation in the basics of retail trading, understanding the various financial markets, the instruments available for trade, the dynamics that drive market movements, and the psychological aspects that influence trader behaviour. This groundwork is essential for developing effective trading strategies and risk management techniques discussed in subsequent chapters.

Chapter 2: The Fundamentals of Risk Management

Section 2.1 The Concept of Risk in Trading

Understanding Risk in Trading

In the world of trading, risk is an ever-present companion to every decision and transaction. It is the potential for financial loss that accompanies every trade. However, risk is not just a harbinger of potential financial downturns; it is also the flip side of the profit potential. Essentially, risk and reward are two sides of the same coin in the financial markets.

Types of Trading Risk

1. **Market Risk (Systematic Risk):** This type of risk is inherent in the market and can be influenced by geopolitical events, economic indicators, and other external factors. It affects a wide range of assets and is difficult to avoid completely.
2. **Credit Risk (Counterparty Risk):** The risk that the other party in a trade may not fulfill their obligations. This is particularly relevant in direct lending or in derivative contracts.
3. **Liquidity Risk:** The risk that you may not be able to buy or sell an asset quickly enough to prevent a loss (or make the intended profit).

Risk-Reward Ratio

One of the fundamental concepts in trading risk management is the risk-reward ratio. It is a measure used by traders to compare the expected returns of an investment to the amount of risk undertaken to capture these returns. For example, a risk-reward ratio of 1:3 means you're risking $1 to make $3, indicating a potentially profitable trade-off if the risk is managed properly.

Managing Risk

Effective risk management involves identifying, assessing, and responding to risk factors throughout the trading process. It requires a clear understanding of one's risk tolerance and the implementation of strategies such as diversification, the use of stop-loss orders, and the careful selection of investment positions based on thorough market analysis.

Examples of Risk Management

- **Diversification:** Spreading investments across various financial instruments, industries, and other categories to reduce exposure to any single asset or risk.
- **Stop-Loss Orders:** Setting predetermined selling points to automatically exit positions at a specified price to limit potential losses.
- **Position Sizing:** Determining how much of your capital to allocate to a single trade based on your risk tolerance and market assessment.

Conclusion

Grasping the concept of risk is crucial for every trader, from novices to seasoned investors. By understanding the types of risk and employing strategic risk management techniques, traders can protect their investments and position themselves for potential gains. It's not about avoiding risk entirely—which is impossible—but about making informed decisions that balance the potential for profit against the tolerance for loss.

Section 2.2 Types of Risks in Trading

Market Risk
Definition: Market risk, also known as systematic risk, refers to the potential for investors to experience losses due to factors that affect the overall performance of the financial markets.

Example: Consider a geopolitical event that triggers uncertainty across global markets. This event might cause a broad sell-off in equities, impacting all stocks regardless of individual company fundamentals.

Management Strategy: Diversification across different asset classes (stocks, bonds, real estate, etc.) can mitigate market risk, as not all assets will respond in the same way to market events.

Credit Risk

Definition: Credit risk arises when there is a possibility that a counterparty in a trade or investment will fail to meet their financial obligations, leading to financial loss for the investor.

Example: If a bond issuer faces financial difficulties and cannot pay the interest or principal, bondholders face credit risk.

Management Strategy: Conduct thorough due diligence on counterparties and diversify holdings across issuers and sectors to reduce exposure to any single entity's credit risk.

Liquidity Risk

Definition: Liquidity risk involves the risk of being unable to quickly sell an asset at its current value due to a lack of buyers or an inefficient market.

Example: Owning a large position in a small-cap stock with low daily trading volume might make it difficult to sell the position without significantly impacting the stock's price.

Management Strategy: Focus on assets with higher liquidity and be mindful of position sizing to ensure you can exit positions without materially affecting the market price.

Operational Risk

Definition: Operational risk is associated with internal failures such as systems malfunctions, human error, or disruptions caused by external events that affect a company's operations.

Example: A trading platform experiences a technical outage during market hours, preventing traders from executing trades or managing positions.

Management Strategy: Employ robust risk management systems, conduct regular audits, and have contingency plans in place to address potential operational disruptions.

Psychological Risk

Definition: Psychological risk refers to the impact of emotional decision-making on trading, where traders might deviate from their strategy based on fear, greed, or other emotional responses.

Example: A trader might hold onto a losing position longer than planned, hoping it will turn around, rather than accepting a loss and adhering to their stop-loss strategy.

Management Strategy: Develop a disciplined trading plan with clear rules for entry, exit, and risk management. Regularly review trades to identify emotional patterns that negatively impact decisions and work on strategies to mitigate these responses.

Each type of risk presents unique challenges to traders, requiring a tailored approach to management and mitigation. By understanding these risks and incorporating strategies to address them, traders can better protect their investments and position themselves for long-term success in the markets.

-

Section 2.3 The Importance of Risk Management in Preserving Capital

Understanding Risk Management

Risk management in trading is a systematic approach to identifying, assessing, and mitigating financial loss in investment decisions. It's the cornerstone of a successful trading strategy because it helps preserve capital—ensuring traders can continue operating in the market over the long term.

Strategies for Minimizing Losses

1. **Setting Stop-Loss Orders**: A stop-loss order is an automatic order to sell an asset when it reaches a certain price, limiting potential losses. For example, if you buy a stock at $100, setting a stop-loss order at $90 limits your loss to 10%.
2. **Diversifying Investments**: Diversification spreads risk across various assets, sectors, or geographical locations. If one investment performs poorly, the others in your portfolio can offset the loss, reducing the overall risk.

3. **Regularly Reviewing and Adjusting Trading Plans**: Market conditions change, and a flexible trading plan can adapt to those changes. Regular reviews allow traders to adjust their strategies based on current market analysis and economic indicators.

Protecting Capital Against the Unexpected

The primary goal of risk management is to protect your capital against unforeseen market movements and losses. This involves careful planning, disciplined execution of trading strategies, and continuous learning. By managing risk effectively, traders can minimize losses, capitalize on opportunities for growth, and achieve sustainable trading practices.

Sustainable Trading Practices

Sustainable trading practices involve not only the technical aspects of managing investments but also developing the psychological resilience to deal with market volatility. This includes maintaining a long-term perspective, avoiding emotional trading decisions, and continuously educating oneself on market trends and risk management techniques.

By incorporating these strategies into your trading approach, you can create a robust framework for managing risk and preserving capital, setting the foundation for long-term success in the financial markets.

Section 2.4 Implementing Risk Management Strategies

Implementing risk management strategies is crucial for the sustainability and success of trading activities. This process involves several key steps, each designed to help traders minimize losses and optimize gains. Here's a detailed guide:

Assessing Risk Tolerance
1. **Personal Assessment**: Begin by understanding your financial situation, goals, and how much risk you can afford to take. This involves evaluating your investment capital, income stability, and emotional capacity to handle market volatility.
2. **Risk Tolerance Questionnaire**: Utilize questionnaires or tools provided by financial advisors or online platforms to quantify your risk tolerance level.

Setting Risk-Reward Ratios
1. **Understanding Risk-Reward Ratio**: This ratio helps traders evaluate the potential reward of an investment against its risk. For instance, a 1:3 ratio means risking $1 to potentially gain $3.
2. **Application in Trades**: Before executing any trade, calculate the expected risk-reward ratio. Ensure it aligns with your trading strategy and risk tolerance.

Using Analytical Tools for Risk Identification
1. **Technical Analysis Tools**: Use charting software to identify potential risk factors such as support and resistance levels, which can inform stop-loss orders.

2. **Fundamental Analysis**: Stay informed on economic indicators, earnings reports, and other fundamental factors that could impact your trades.

Incorporating Risk Management into Daily Trading

1. **Daily Limits**: Set daily loss limits to protect your capital. If you hit this limit, stop trading for the day to reassess your strategy.
2. **Stop-Loss and Take-Profit Orders**: Utilize these orders to automatically close positions once they reach a certain price level, locking in profits or preventing further losses.

Practical Examples

- **Example 1**: A trader buys shares at $50 each, setting a stop-loss order at $45 and a take-profit order at $60, establishing a clear exit strategy for both scenarios.
- **Example 2**: Using diversification, a trader spreads their investment across stocks, bonds, and commodities. This reduces the impact of a poor performance in any single asset class on the overall portfolio.

Adapting to Market Conditions

- **Regular Review**: Constantly review and adjust your trading plan based on market performance and personal trading results. This might involve adjusting your risk tolerance and strategies as you gain more experience.
- **Continued Education**: Keep learning about new risk management tools and strategies. The financial markets are always evolving, and staying informed is key to adapting your approach.

Conclusion

Implementing effective risk management strategies is not a one-time task but a continuous process that requires diligence, education, and adaptability. By following the steps outlined above and using practical examples as a guide, traders can develop a disciplined approach to risk management, helping to safeguard investments and achieve long-term growth in the volatile world of trading.

Section 2.5 Risk Management Tools and Techniques

In the pursuit of successful trading, understanding and implementing risk management tools and techniques is crucial. This section explores a variety of methods traders can use to mitigate risk, enhance decision-making, and protect investments.

Traditional Methods

Stop-Loss Orders: A stop-loss order is an essential tool for managing risk. It automatically closes out a trading position at a predetermined price level, preventing further losses. For instance, if a stock is bought at $100, a stop-loss might be set at $90 to limit potential loss to $10 per share.

Diversification: Spreading investments across different asset classes (stocks, bonds, commodities) or within the same asset class (different sectors or geographies) can reduce risk. Diversification helps mitigate the impact of poor performance in any single investment.

Advanced Techniques

Hedging: Hedging involves taking an offsetting or opposite position in a related asset to protect against price movements. For example, options contracts can be used to hedge stock positions, providing the right to buy or sell at predetermined prices.

Using Derivatives for Risk Protection: Derivatives like options and futures can be strategic tools for risk management. They allow traders to speculate on the future price of an asset without directly owning it, offering a way to hedge or to limit potential losses.

Automation and Software

Risk Management Software: Various software platforms offer comprehensive tools for risk analysis, including volatility assessment, correlation tracking, and portfolio stress-testing. These platforms can automate many risk management processes, providing real-time data and analytics.

Trading Platforms with Integrated Risk Tools: Many trading platforms now incorporate advanced risk management features directly into their interface. Features may include automatic stop-loss and take-profit orders, risk-reward ratio calculators, and margin calculators.

Applications for Real-Time Data and Analytics: Access to real-time market data and analytics is vital for making informed trading decisions. Applications like Bloomberg Terminal or Reuters Eikon provide extensive data, news, and analytics tools, though they come at a premium price.

Practical Example

Imagine a trader who diversifies their portfolio across technology stocks, government bonds, and gold. They use stop-loss orders to protect each position, set based on a 2% threshold from the buying price. For additional protection against market volatility, they hedge their stock positions by purchasing put options. Using a trading platform with integrated risk tools, they monitor their portfolio's performance, making adjustments based on real-time analytics and changing market conditions.

By leveraging these risk management tools and techniques, traders can create a more resilient trading strategy. While risk can never be entirely eliminated, these methods provide a framework for managing it effectively, aiming to preserve capital and maximize potential returns over the long term.

Section 2.6 Building a Risk-Aware Trading Mindset

Understanding the Risk-Aware Mindset

A risk-aware mindset in trading is about more than just safeguarding assets; it's about integrating risk management into every decision, balancing the pursuit of rewards against the potential for loss. This mindset is crucial for long-term success and sustainability in trading.

Maintaining Discipline

Discipline is the cornerstone of a risk-aware mindset. It involves:

- **Setting clear rules** for when to enter and exit trades, based on thorough research and analysis rather than impulse or emotion.
- **Adhering to a trading plan**, even in volatile markets, to avoid making decisions based on fear or greed.

Avoiding Common Pitfalls

- **Overtrading**: Entering too many trades without proper analysis can deplete capital through fees and losses. To avoid this, set a limit on the number of trades per day or week based on your strategy and review each trade's rationale.
- **Chasing Losses**: Trying to recover losses by doubling down on new trades can lead to greater losses. Recognize when to step back and reassess your strategy.

Staying Focused on Long-Term Objectives

- Long-term success in trading comes from consistent performance over time, not from one-off gains. Focus on achieving steady growth and learning from both successes and failures.

Psychological Aspects of Trading

Understanding the psychological pressures of trading is essential. Feelings of anxiety or excitement can cloud judgment, leading traders to deviate from their strategies. Techniques such as mindfulness, meditation, or simply taking breaks can help manage these emotions.

Practical Steps to Build a Risk-Aware Mindset

1. **Educate Yourself**: Continuously learn about market trends, analysis techniques, and risk management strategies. Knowledge is a powerful tool against uncertainty.
2. **Use Risk Management Tools**: Leverage stop-loss orders, diversification, and other tools discussed earlier to help automate and enforce discipline in your trading decisions.
3. **Review and Reflect**: Regularly review your trades to understand what worked and what didn't. Use this insight to refine your approach, focusing on decision-making processes rather than just outcomes.
4. **Seek Feedback**: Engage with a community of traders or a mentor who can provide constructive feedback on your trading strategy and mindset.

By fostering a risk-aware mindset, traders can navigate the markets more effectively, making informed decisions that balance the potential for profit against the risk of loss. This approach not only preserves capital but also contributes to the psychological well-being and long-term success of the trader.

Chapter 3: Setting Up for Success

Section 3.1 Creating a Trading Plan

3.1.1 Setting Clear, Achievable Goals

When setting goals for your trading plan, consider both your long-term financial objectives and what you aim to achieve in the short term. Goals should be specific, measurable, achievable, relevant, and time-bound (SMART). For example, a realistic goal could be to achieve a 20% return on your investment portfolio within a year through day trading and swing trading strategies.

3.1.2 Defining Risk Tolerance

Risk tolerance varies greatly among traders and is influenced by your financial situation, investment experience, and even your emotional capacity to handle losses. Assessing your risk tolerance involves considering how much capital you can afford to lose, how fluctuations in your trading account's value affect you emotionally, and your overall investment horizon. Tools like questionnaires or discussions with a financial advisor can help clarify your risk tolerance level.

3.1.3 Developing Strategies

The core of your trading plan will be the strategies you employ, which should align with your goals and risk tolerance. These strategies can be based on:

- **Fundamental Analysis**: Analysing economic indicators, company earnings, and industry trends to make trading decisions.
- **Technical Analysis**: Using price charts and patterns to predict future price movements.

For instance, if your risk tolerance is low, you might focus on conservative strategies, such as investing in blue-chip stocks or using options for hedging. Conversely, if you're more risk-tolerant and looking for higher returns, you might explore volatile markets like forex or cryptocurrencies, employing strategies like scalping or high-frequency trading.

Adjusting Your Trading Plan

As you gain more experience and the market conditions change, revisiting and adjusting your trading plan is crucial. This might involve refining your goals, adapting your risk tolerance based on new financial circumstances, or experimenting with different trading strategies as you learn what works best for you.

While this overview provides a framework for creating a trading plan, successful trading requires continuous learning, discipline, and the willingness to adapt to changing market dynamics.

Let's create a hypothetical example based on the framework for creating a trading plan as outlined:

Example Trading Plan for Alex, a Novice Retail Trader

3.1.1 Setting Clear, Achievable Goals

- **Short-term Goal**: To learn the basics of stock market trading and execute at least one trade per week using a demo account for the first three months.
- **Long-term Goal**: To achieve a 15% return on the initial investment within the first year of trading real money by focusing on swing trading in the technology sector.

3.1.2 Defining Risk Tolerance

After completing several online risk tolerance questionnaires and reflecting on personal financial situations, Alex determines that a moderate risk tolerance level is appropriate. This is based on:

- An available trading capital of $5,000 that Alex is willing to invest, understanding that it's money Alex can afford to lose without affecting his financial stability.
- A preference to avoid high-volatility instruments like cryptocurrencies in favour of more stable stocks.

3.1.3 Developing Strategies

Given Alex's goals and risk tolerance, the following strategies are chosen:

- **For the Learning Phase with a Demo Account**: Focus on technical analysis, learning to read charts, understand trends, and practice with stocks in the technology sector since they hold personal interest and growth potential.

- **Transition to Real Money Trading**: Begin with swing trading strategies, leveraging technical analysis to find entry and exit points over several days to weeks. Investments will be limited to 2% of the total capital per trade to manage risk.

Adjusting the Plan

- After the initial three months, Alex plans to review the performance in the demo account, focusing on the success rate of trades and the ability to stick to the planned strategy without letting emotions dictate decisions.
- If the demo trading phase shows consistent success, Alex will start trading with real money, initially with a smaller amount ($1,000) to test the emotional response to potential losses and gains.
- Quarterly reviews will be scheduled to assess performance, with a particular focus on whether the 15% return goal is realistic and if the risk management strategies effectively protect the capital.

This example illustrates how a novice trader can structure their approach to entering the trading world, balancing educational goals with risk management to lay a foundation for potential long-term success.

I can offer a general framework that an advanced trader with significant capital, such as $100,000, might consider when crafting a comprehensive trading plan.

Example Trading Plan for Jordan, an Advanced Retail Trader

Goal Setting

- **Short-term Goals**: Jordan aims to leverage advanced trading techniques such as algorithmic trading and options strategies to exploit short-term market inefficiencies, targeting a 5% return on capital within the first quarter.
- **Long-term Goals**: Over the year, Jordan seeks a 20% return on the investment by diversifying across different asset classes, including equities, fixed income, commodities, and potentially cryptocurrencies, depending on market conditions.

Risk Tolerance Assessment

Given the substantial trading capital, Jordan has determined a moderate to high risk tolerance but wishes to ensure capital preservation as a priority. This involves:

- Allocating a maximum of 10% of the portfolio to high-risk ventures such as cryptocurrency trading or speculative options plays.
- Using a tiered approach to risk, where the bulk of the portfolio (60%) is dedicated to more stable, long-term investments, and the remainder is allocated to medium and high-risk strategies.

Developing Strategies

- **Algorithmic Trading**: Jordan plans to use a portion of the capital to develop and deploy algorithmic trading strategies that can automatically execute trades based on predefined criteria, aiming to capture small, consistent profits.
- **Options Trading**: Utilizing advanced options strategies like iron condors or straddles to generate income in flat or volatile markets, respectively, dedicating 20% of the trading capital to options.
- **Diversification and Hedging**: To protect against market downturns, Jordan will diversify the investment portfolio across different asset classes and use derivatives as a hedging tool to manage potential losses.

Adjustments and Review

- Jordan commits to a monthly review of the trading strategies' performance, with particular attention to the algorithmic strategies' effectiveness and the options portfolio's risk-adjusted returns.
- Ready to adjust the trading plan based on evolving market conditions, Jordan will rebalance the portfolio quarterly to maintain the desired risk level and capitalize on new opportunities.

In this scenario, an advanced trader like Jordan uses a mix of sophisticated trading techniques and prudent risk management to aim for substantial returns while protecting the invested capital. Regular review and adaptability are key components of the trading plan, allowing Jordan to navigate the complexities of various market environments effectively.

3.2 Importance of a Trading Journal

3.2.1 What to Include in Your Journal: A trading journal should comprehensively document each trade to serve as a historical record and a tool for reflection and learning. Essential elements to include are:

- **Entry and Exit Points**: Document the price points at which you entered and exited each trade.
- **Trade Size**: Note the volume of shares or contracts traded.
- **Rationale Behind Each Trade**: Write down the reasons for making the trade, including any technical indicators used, fundamental analysis, or market conditions that influenced your decision.
- **Outcome**: Record the profit or loss from the trade.
- **Emotional State**: Jot down how you felt before, during, and after the trade, as emotions can significantly impact decision-making.

3.2.2 Analysing Your Trades: Regularly review your trading journal to identify patterns or tendencies in your trading behaviour. Look for:

- **Successful Strategies**: Identify what worked well and consider how to apply these strategies more broadly.

- **Common Mistakes**: Pinpoint recurring errors or misjudgments to avoid in the future.
- **Emotional Triggers**: Recognize situations that lead to emotional trading, such as fear or greed, and develop strategies to mitigate these responses.

3.2.3 Refining Your Strategies: Use insights gained from your journal to refine and evolve your trading strategies. This could involve:

- **Adjusting Risk Management Techniques**: If you find you're consistently hitting stop-loss points, consider whether you need to adjust your risk tolerance or entry/exit criteria.
- **Experimenting with New Strategies**: Use the journal to track the performance of new strategies on a small scale before fully integrating them into your trading plan.
- **Improving Discipline**: Commit to sticking to your trading plan more strictly, using the journal as a accountability tool.

A trading journal is more than a record; it's a tool for continuous self-improvement and learning in the dynamic world of trading. By diligently documenting and reviewing each trade, traders can gain valuable insights into their own habits and market trends, enabling them to make more informed decisions and refine their strategies for greater success.

This structure aims to provide a comprehensive overview of how to effectively use a trading journal to improve trading practices and decision-making processes.

Example 1: Entry for a Successful Trade

- **Date**: September 15, 2023
- **Entry Point**: Bought 100 shares of XYZ Corp at $50 per share.
- **Exit Point**: Sold 100 shares of XYZ Corp at $55 per share.
- **Trade Size**: $5,000 (100 shares * $50/share)
- **Rationale**: Technical analysis indicated a breakout above the 50-day moving average, suggesting an upward trend. Positive earnings reports from XYZ Corp also boosted confidence.
- **Outcome**: Profit of $500 (excluding transaction fees).
- **Emotional State**: Confident at entry due to strong indicators; experienced anxiety before deciding to sell but ultimately relied on predetermined exit strategy.
- **Adjustments/Notes for Future Trades**: The strategy worked well for this trade, reaffirming the importance of exit points based on technical indicators. Consider increasing trade size for similar future setups with strong signals.

Example 2: Entry for a Trade with a Loss

- **Date**: October 10, 2023
- **Entry Point**: Bought 50 shares of ABC Tech at $100 per share.
- **Exit Point**: Sold 50 shares of ABC Tech at $95 per share due to stop-loss order.
- **Trade Size**: $5,000 (50 shares * $100/share)

- **Rationale**: Entered the trade expecting a rebound from support levels around $100, influenced by past performance and sector growth.
- **Outcome**: Loss of $250 (excluding transaction fees).
- **Emotional State**: Initially optimistic based on historical performance; however, felt disappointment after stop-loss was hit. Recognized the value of stop-loss in preventing larger losses.
- **Adjustments/Notes for Future Trades**: Review the criteria for selecting stocks based on support levels. Increase emphasis on current market conditions and broader sector performance. Reassess risk tolerance and consider adjusting stop-loss strategy to allow more room for normal price fluctuations.

These examples illustrate how a trading journal can serve as a reflective tool, enabling traders to analyse their decisions, understand their emotional responses, and refine their strategies based on real trading experiences.

Section 3.3 Selecting the Right Brokerage and Trading Tools

3.3.1 Factors to Consider When Choosing a Brokerage

When evaluating brokerages, consider their:

- **Commission Fees and Other Charges**: Compare the costs of trading, including spreads, commission fees, and any hidden charges that might affect your trading profitability.
- **Platform Usability**: Choose a platform that matches your technical skills and trading style. It should provide easy access to market data, fast execution, and stability.
- **Customer Service Quality**: Ensure the brokerage offers reliable support with quick response times and knowledgeable staff.
- **Account Types and Accessibility**: Verify the brokerage offers account types that suit your trading needs, including margin accounts if you plan to trade on leverage.
- **Regulatory Compliance**: Check that the brokerage is regulated by a reputable authority to ensure your funds are secure.

3.3.2 Essential Trading Tools

Your trading toolkit should include:

- **Charting Software**: Tools like TradingView or MetaTrader offer advanced charting capabilities, technical indicators, and analytical tools for market analysis.
- **Risk Management Calculators**: Utilize calculators for assessing risk-reward ratios, position sizing based on your capital, and stop-loss/take-profit levels.
- **Real-time News Feeds**: Stay informed with platforms that provide real-time news and economic event alerts to react quickly to market changes.

3.3.3 Leveraging Technology for Success

- **Automated Trading Systems**: Consider whether the brokerage supports automated trading for executing strategies based on predefined criteria without manual intervention.
- **Mobile Trading**: Ensure the platform offers a robust mobile app that allows you to monitor and execute trades securely from anywhere.
- **API Access**: Advanced traders might require API access for custom strategies and integration with third-party tools for enhanced analysis and trading automation.

By carefully considering these factors, you can select a brokerage and set of trading tools that will support your trading activities effectively, helping you to manage risk and capitalize on market opportunities more efficiently.

This guidance aims to help you understand the critical elements in choosing the right brokerage and trading tools, enhancing your ability to write a detailed and informative section for your book.
I Will create hypothetical examples based on the structured guide provided for selecting the right brokerage and trading tools:

Example 1: Choosing a Brokerage

Scenario: Alex is an experienced day trader focusing on forex and commodities. Alex looks for a brokerage that offers:

- **Low Commission Fees**: To maximize profits from frequent trades.

- **Highly Usable Platform**: With real-time charting and quick execution capabilities.
- **Robust Customer Service**: To quickly resolve any issues given the fast-paced trading environment.

Brokerage Choice: Alex decides on "TradeFast Pro", a brokerage known for its competitive spreads in forex and commodities, and a state-of-the-art trading platform that includes advanced charting tools, real-time data, and rapid trade execution. "TradeFast Pro" is also praised for its 24/7 customer service, which is crucial for day traders who operate in various market hours.

Example 2: Essential Trading Tools

Scenario: Sarah, a swing trader focusing on stocks and ETFs, needs tools to analyse market trends and manage risk effectively.

- **Charting Software**: Sarah uses "ChartMaster 360", which offers comprehensive charting options, numerous technical indicators, and customizability for detailed analysis.
- **Risk Management Calculator**: She utilizes "RiskShield Tool", which helps calculate the ideal position size based on her account balance and risk tolerance, ensuring she never risks more than 2% of her capital on a single trade.
- **Real-time News Feed**: Sarah subscribes to "MarketPulse News", providing her with instant updates on economic events and stock market news, helping her make informed decisions quickly.

Example 3: Leveraging Technology for Success

Scenario: Chris, an algorithmic trader, requires advanced technology to develop and execute complex trading strategies.

- **Automated Trading System**: Chris uses "AlgoTrader Pro", a platform that supports custom algorithm development and back-testing, allowing him to refine his strategies based on historical data.
- **Mobile Trading App**: He relies on "TradeOnTheGo", a mobile app that offers full functionality of his desktop trading environment, ensuring he can monitor and adjust his trades anytime, anywhere.
- **API Access**: Chris benefits from API access provided by his brokerage, "Quantum Brokers", enabling him to connect his custom-built analytics tools directly with his trading account for seamless data analysis and trade execution.

These examples illustrate how traders with different focuses and strategies might select brokerages and tools that best suit their specific needs, highlighting the importance of factors such as fees, platform usability, customer service, and the availability of advanced technology and trading tools.

I will provide one real world example.

For example, **Interactive Brokers** is often cited for its advanced trading platform, competitive commission rates, and extensive access to international markets, making it a preferred choice for traders looking for flexibility and a wide range of instruments. Their platform provides powerful analysis tools, real-time data, and risk management features designed to cater to both novice and seasoned traders.

Another example is **TD Ameritrade**, known for its thinkorswim trading platform, which offers robust charting and analysis tools, paper trading options, and a user-friendly interface. They provide comprehensive educational resources to help traders develop their skills and strategies.

These examples illustrate the type of brokerage features that can significantly impact trading efficiency and success. Always consider your specific trading needs, preferences, and goals when choosing a brokerage and trading tools.

Chapter 4: Key Risk Management Techniques

Section 4.1 Position Sizing and Money Management Strategies

4.1.1 Understanding Position Sizing

Position sizing is a critical aspect of risk management in trading. It involves determining the amount of capital to risk on any single trade relative to the total trading capital available. The goal of position sizing is to maximize potential returns while limiting the risk of significant losses. Proper position sizing ensures that a few bad trades won't significantly impact the overall trading capital.

Why It Matters: Position sizing directly affects your trading risk by controlling the amount of capital at stake. It helps in maintaining a balanced portfolio and prevents overexposure to any single trade.

4.1.2 Money Management Strategies

Effective money management is foundational for successful trading. It encompasses not just how much to risk on each trade but also how to allocate resources across different trades and strategies.

- **Percentage Risk Model**: This model involves risking a fixed percentage of your total capital on each trade. For example, if your capital is $10,000 and you choose to risk 2% per trade, you would risk $200 on each trade.
- **Fixed Dollar Amount Model**: Here, a trader risks the same dollar amount on every trade. This method is straightforward but does not adjust for changes in total capital over time.
- **Kelly Criterion**: This formula calculates the optimal amount to risk based on your past trading performance, specifically the win rate and the win/loss ratio. It aims to maximize capital growth by dynamically adjusting position sizes.

Diversification of Trades: Spreading capital across various trades or strategies can reduce risk. Diversification ensures that the impact of a losing trade is minimized relative to the overall portfolio.

Setting Capital Limits: Establishing maximum capital limits for specific strategies or markets can protect against significant losses in volatile or high-risk areas.

4.1.3 Tools and Calculators

Several tools and calculators can aid traders in applying these position sizing and money management strategies effectively:

- **Risk Management Calculators**: These calculators help traders determine the appropriate position size based on the percentage risk model or other strategies, taking into account the account balance, risk percentage, stop loss, and the instrument's price.
- **Kelly Criterion Calculator**: This tool calculates the optimal bet size to maximize the growth rate of capital based on the trader's past performance metrics.
- **Diversification Analysis Tools**: Software that analyses the correlation between different assets in a portfolio, helping traders to diversify effectively.

By incorporating these position sizing and money management strategies, traders can create a more resilient trading approach. These methods help in protecting the trading capital from significant losses, enabling traders to participate in the market more confidently and with a higher potential for profit over the long term.

Creating detailed, real-world examples based on the previously outlined section on position sizing and money management strategies involves synthesizing general market knowledge with hypothetical scenarios. Here are some illustrative examples:

Real-World Examples of Position Sizing and Money Management Strategies

Example 1: Percentage Risk Model in Action
Scenario: Taylor has a trading account balance of $20,000 and decides to risk 1% of their capital on each trade.

Application: For a trade on stock XYZ, Taylor calculates the risk as $200 (1% of $20,000). If the entry price for XYZ is $50 and Taylor sets a stop-loss at $48, the risk per share is $2. Using the risk amount ($200) and the risk per share ($2), Taylor decides to buy 100 shares of XYZ. This position sizing ensures that even if the trade hits the stop-loss, the total loss will not exceed 1% of the trading account.

Example 2: Fixed Dollar Amount Model
Scenario: Jordan, a trader with a $50,000 portfolio, chooses to risk a fixed amount of $500 on each trade.

Application: When considering a trade on ABC stock, Jordan determines that the risk per share from the entry point to the stop-loss is $5. By dividing the fixed risk amount ($500) by the risk per share ($5), Jordan calculates the position size as 100 shares of ABC. This strategy simplifies decision-making and ensures consistent risk management across trades.

Example 3: Using the Kelly Criterion for Optimal Bet Size

Scenario: Alex, an experienced forex trader, has determined through historical performance analysis that their winning probability is 55% with a win/loss ratio of 2:1.

Application: Applying the Kelly Criterion formula, Alex calculates the optimal fraction of the capital to be risked on each trade. Based on their win rate and win/loss ratio, the Kelly formula suggests that risking approximately 10% of the capital on each trade maximizes the growth rate of Alex's trading account. This aggressive strategy is balanced by Alex's proven track record and the high win rate.

Example 4: Diversification Analysis Tool

Scenario: Sam uses a diversification analysis tool to manage a portfolio of stocks, bonds, and commodities.

Application: The tool indicates that Sam's current portfolio is heavily correlated with technology stocks, posing a higher risk if the tech sector experiences a downturn. To mitigate this risk, Sam adjusts the portfolio by reducing exposure to technology stocks and increasing investments in bonds and commodities, which historically have a low correlation with the tech sector. This diversification helps in spreading risk and protecting the portfolio from sector-specific downturns.

Tools and Calculators

Risk Management Calculators: Traders like Taylor and Jordan use online risk management calculators to quickly determine the appropriate position size for each trade, ensuring their risk parameters are consistently applied.

Kelly Criterion Calculator: Advanced traders like Alex might use specialized software that incorporates the Kelly Criterion into its calculations, helping to optimize capital allocation based on historical performance data.

These examples illustrate the practical application of position sizing and money management strategies in various trading scenarios, highlighting the importance of systematic risk management in preserving capital and maximizing profits.

Section 4.2 Setting Stop-Loss Orders and Take-Profit Levels

4.2.1 The Importance of Stop-Loss Orders

Stop-loss orders are essential tools for risk management, acting as a safety net to automatically exit a trade at a predetermined loss threshold. This tool is crucial for preserving capital by preventing larger, unmanageable losses if the market moves against your position.

- **How They Work**: A stop-loss order is set at a specific price level. If the market price hits this level, the order is triggered, and the trade is closed at the next available price, minimizing further losses.
- **Critical Component**: Incorporating stop-loss orders into your trading plan helps enforce discipline, removing emotional decision-making and ensuring that losses are kept within acceptable limits.

4.2.2 Setting Take-Profit Levels

Take-profit levels allow traders to lock in profits by setting an automatic exit point for a trade when it reaches a specified profit threshold.

- **Strategies**: Setting these levels requires analysing historical data, current market conditions, and your financial goals. A common approach is to set take-profit levels at key resistance levels for long positions or support levels for short positions.
- **Aligning with Goals**: Your take-profit levels should reflect your trading strategy's objectives, whether securing quick, small gains in scalping or aiming for larger returns in swing trading.

4.2.3 Balancing Risk and Reward

Finding the right balance between risk and reward is pivotal in trading. This balance is achieved by setting appropriate stop-loss and take-profit levels that reflect your risk tolerance and trading goals.

- **Techniques**: Utilize risk-reward ratios to guide the placement of stop-loss and take-profit orders. For example, a 1:3 risk-reward ratio means for every dollar risked, three dollars are targeted as potential profit.
- **Practical Application**: If entering a trade at $100 with a stop-loss at $95 (risking $5), set a take-profit level at $115 to maintain a 1:3 risk-reward ratio. This strategy ensures that profits are maximized relative to potential losses, contributing to overall trading success over time.

Example of Practical Application:

Imagine a trader who buys a stock at $50, aiming for a conservative trading approach. They might set a stop-loss order at $47.50 (risking $2.50 per share) and a take-profit level at $55 (aiming for a $5 gain per share). This setup creates a risk-reward ratio of 1:2, aligning with the trader's moderate risk tolerance and goal of steady capital growth.

This section emphasizes the strategic importance of stop-loss orders and take-profit levels in safeguarding investments and securing profits. By meticulously planning these thresholds, traders can effectively manage risk, ensure discipline, and optimize their trading outcomes.

Section 4.3 Diversification Across Instruments and Asset Classes

4.3.1 Principles of Diversification

Diversification stands as a cornerstone in the realm of risk management, founded on the maxim that one should not put all their eggs in one basket. This principle is rooted in the idea of spreading investments across a wide range of assets to mitigate the risk of significant losses if one investment underperforms.

- **Risk Reduction**: By investing in a variety of asset classes, sectors, and geographical regions, traders can reduce unsystematic risk—the risk associated with a specific company or industry.

- **Portfolio Volatility**: Diversification helps in smoothing out returns over time, as the negative performance of some investments is likely to be offset by positive performance in others, reducing overall portfolio volatility.

4.3.2 Diversification Strategies

Effective diversification involves more than just owning different assets. It requires strategic planning and understanding of how different investments interact with each other.

- **Across Asset Classes**: Spread your investments across stocks, bonds, commodities, and possibly cryptocurrencies. Each asset class responds differently to market conditions. For example, bonds often act as a counterbalance to stocks, providing stability when equity markets are volatile.
- **Within Asset Classes**: Diversify within asset classes by investing in various sectors, industries, or countries. For instance, within the stock portion of your portfolio, consider a mix of technology, healthcare, finance, and consumer goods from both domestic and international markets.
- **Alternative Investments**: Including assets like real estate or collectibles can offer further diversification benefits, as their performance is often uncorrelated with traditional financial markets.

4.3.3 Assessing Diversification Effectiveness

Evaluating the effectiveness of your diversification strategy is crucial to ensure it aligns with your risk tolerance and investment goals.

- **Portfolio Analysis Tools**: Use tools that analyse your portfolio's overall risk, return, and correlation among assets. These tools can highlight areas where your portfolio may be overexposed to a single risk factor.
- **Rebalancing**: Regularly review and adjust your portfolio to maintain your desired level of diversification. This may involve selling off assets that have grown to constitute too large a portion of your portfolio and reinvesting the proceeds in underrepresented assets.
- **Market Conditions**: Stay informed about changing market conditions that might affect the correlation between different asset classes. What worked in the past may not work in the future, requiring adjustments to your diversification strategy.

Example of a Diversified Portfolio:

Imagine an investor named Alex, who has a moderate risk tolerance and a long-term investment horizon. Alex's diversified portfolio might look something like this:

- **60% Stocks**: Spread across technology, healthcare, consumer goods, and energy sectors, with a mix of domestic and international companies.
- **20% Bonds**: A combination of government and corporate bonds, with varying maturities to hedge against interest rate risks.
- **10% Commodities**: Investments in gold and oil, which can serve as a hedge against inflation and currency devaluation.

- **5% Real Estate**: Through real estate investment trusts (REITs), offering exposure to commercial and residential real estate markets.
- **5% Cash or Cash Equivalents**: Maintained for liquidity and to take advantage of new investment opportunities.

By adhering to these diversification principles and strategies, Alex can effectively manage risk and position the portfolio for balanced growth over time, adapting as necessary to evolving market conditions.

Let's delve into more hypothetical examples that illustrate the principles of diversification in trading and investment strategies:

Example 1: Sector and Industry Diversification

Scenario: Jamie, an equity trader, decides to diversify their portfolio across various sectors to mitigate the risk associated with any single market sector.

- **Before Diversification**: Jamie's portfolio is heavily invested in technology stocks, comprising 70% of the total portfolio.
- **Diversification Strategy**: Jamie reallocates the portfolio to include healthcare (20%), financial services (20%), utilities (10%), and consumer goods (10%), reducing the technology sector's weight to 40%.
- **Outcome**: The diversified portfolio now has exposure to sectors with different economic sensitivities, reducing the impact of a downturn in the tech sector on Jamie's overall portfolio performance.

Example 2: Geographic Diversification

Scenario: Mia, who primarily invests in U.S. stocks, seeks to reduce country-specific risks, especially those related to economic and political factors in the U.S.

- **Before Diversification**: 100% of Mia's stock portfolio is in U.S. companies.
- **Diversification Strategy**: Mia decides to allocate 30% of her portfolio to international markets, including 15% to emerging markets and 15% to developed markets in Europe and Asia.
- **Outcome**: This geographic diversification helps protect Mia's portfolio against U.S.-centric economic downturns, leveraging growth opportunities in other parts of the world.

Example 3: Asset Class Diversification

Scenario: Ethan is concerned about the volatility in the stock market and looks for ways to protect his investments from significant swings.

- **Before Diversification**: Ethan's investments are 90% in stocks and 10% in cash.
- **Diversification Strategy**: Ethan diversifies his portfolio to include 50% stocks, 20% bonds, 10% real estate (through REITs), 10% commodities (gold and oil), and 10% in cash equivalents.
- **Outcome**: The inclusion of bonds and real estate provides steady income and some protection against stock market volatility, while commodities offer a hedge against inflation, creating a more resilient portfolio.

Example 4: Diversification Using Mutual Funds and ETFs

Scenario: Olivia is a novice investor with limited capital but wants a diversified investment portfolio.

- **Before Diversification**: Olivia is unsure how to invest her funds across different asset classes without significant capital.
- **Diversification Strategy**: Olivia invests in a mix of mutual funds and ETFs that cover a broad range of assets, including a total stock market fund, an international fund, a bond index fund, and a commodity ETF.
- **Outcome**: By using mutual funds and ETFs, Olivia achieves broad diversification across thousands of individual securities and various asset classes with a relatively small investment, reducing her portfolio's risk.

These examples showcase the importance and effectiveness of diversification strategies in managing risk and aiming for more stable returns over time, illustrating how diversification principles can be applied in real-world trading and investment scenarios.

Chapter 5: Advanced Risk Management Strategies

Section 5.1 Leveraging Options for Risk Management

5.1.1 Basics of Options Trading

Options are financial derivatives that give the buyer the right, but not the obligation, to buy (call option) or sell (put option) an underlying asset at a specified price (strike price) before a certain date (expiration date). Options trading can serve various purposes, from hedging and managing risk to speculating on future price movements with a predefined risk profile.

- **Call Options**: Give the holder the right to buy the underlying asset. Traders buy call options when they anticipate the asset's price will rise.
- **Put Options**: Allow the holder to sell the underlying asset. Traders use put options to hedge against or speculate on a decline in the asset's price.

5.1.2 Protective Puts and Covered Calls

Protective Puts: This strategy involves buying a put option for an asset you already own. The protective put acts as insurance, setting a floor on the potential losses if the asset's price falls sharply. For example, if you own 100 shares of a stock trading at $50 and buy a put option with a strike price of $45, your potential loss is limited to $5 per share (excluding the cost of the option).

Covered Calls: In a covered call strategy, you own the underlying asset and sell a call option on that asset. This strategy generates income through the option premium, providing some cushion against a decline in the asset's price, but it also caps the potential gains if the asset's price rises above the strike price of the call option. For instance, if you own shares that are currently trading at $50 and sell a call option with a strike price of $55, you keep the premium but will have to sell the shares at $55 if the stock's price exceeds this level before expiration.

5.1.3 Using Options for Speculation

Options can also be used to speculate on the direction of the market with limited risk. The maximum loss on buying an option is the premium paid, making it a popular choice for speculative strategies.

- **Bullish Strategies**: Buying call options to profit from an expected price increase in the underlying asset. The leverage effect of options means a relatively small investment can lead to significant returns if the market moves favourably.
- **Bearish Strategies**: Purchasing put options if you expect the market to decline. This allows traders to profit from downward movements without needing to short sell stocks, which can involve unlimited risks.

Example of Options for Risk Management:

Imagine you own stock in Company XYZ, currently trading at $100, and you're concerned about potential short-term downside risk. To protect your investment, you purchase a put option with a strike price of $95 for a premium of $2 per share. If XYZ's stock falls to $90, your loss on the stock is offset by gains from the put option, effectively limiting your maximum loss to the cost of the premium plus the difference between the stock's current price and the strike price.

Options are a powerful tool in a trader's arsenal, offering flexible strategies for risk management, income generation, and speculative trading with controlled risk. Understanding how to use options effectively can significantly enhance a trader's ability to manage and protect their portfolio.

Section 5.2 Understanding and Using Hedging Techniques

5.2.1 Fundamentals of Hedging

Hedging is a risk management strategy employed to reduce or limit the risk of adverse price movements in an asset. By taking an opposite position in a related asset, traders and investors can protect their investments from downturns in the market. While hedging can safeguard against losses, it's important to note that it can also cap potential gains. The essence of hedging is not to make a profit but to provide security against losses.

- **Importance in Trading and Investment Strategies**: Hedging is crucial for managing the uncertainties of the market. For institutional investors, corporations, and individual traders, hedging techniques can stabilize earnings and preserve capital over the long term.

5.2.2 Hedging with Derivatives

Derivatives are financial instruments whose value is derived from the value of an underlying asset. They are commonly used for hedging purposes because they allow investors to protect their portfolios without needing to liquidate their positions in the underlying asset.

- **Futures Contracts**: Agreements to buy or sell an asset at a future date at a price that is agreed upon today. Traders can use futures to hedge against price changes in the underlying asset.
- **Options Contracts**: Provide the right, but not the obligation, to buy (call option) or sell (put option) an underlying asset at a specified price before a certain date. Options can be used to construct protective strategies for a portfolio.
- **Swaps**: Contracts through which two parties exchange liabilities or cash flows from two different financial instruments. Interest rate swaps can hedge against changes in interest rates affecting the value of a portfolio.

5.2.3 Real-World Hedging Examples
Example 1: Hedging with Futures in Agriculture

A farmer expects to harvest 10,000 bushels of wheat in three months and is concerned about a potential decline in wheat prices. To hedge against this risk, the farmer sells wheat futures contracts equivalent to the harvest size at today's prices. If wheat prices fall by the time of the harvest, the loss in the cash market (actual selling price of the wheat) is offset by gains in the futures market.

Example 2: Hedging a Stock Portfolio with Options

An investor holds a diversified stock portfolio valued at $1,000,000 and is worried about a short-term downturn in the stock market. To hedge this portfolio, the investor buys put options on a stock market index that closely tracks the performance of their portfolio. If the market falls, the increase in the value of the put options compensates for losses in the portfolio's value.

Example 3: Hedging Interest Rate Risk with Swaps

A company with a floating rate term loan is exposed to the risk of rising interest rates, which would increase their financing costs. To hedge this risk, the company enters into an interest rate swap agreement, where it agrees to pay a fixed rate to a counterparty in exchange for receiving a floating rate. This swap locks in the cost of the company's borrowing, protecting it from future interest rate increases.

Through these examples, it's evident that hedging is a versatile tool for managing financial risks. Whether dealing with commodities, stock portfolios, or interest rate changes, effectively applied hedging strategies can protect against unfavourable market movements, ensuring more predictable financial outcomes.

Section 5.3 Risk Management in Algorithmic Trading

5.3.1 Introduction to Algorithmic Trading

Algorithmic trading involves the use of computer algorithms to execute trades automatically at high speed based on predetermined criteria. This method of trading relies on complex models and formulas to make decisions, aiming to capture profit opportunities faster than human traders can. Unlike traditional trading, which is often influenced by human emotions and subjective judgment, algorithmic trading seeks efficiency and speed, leveraging data analysis and patterns in the market.

- **Advantages**: Includes the ability to execute orders at the best possible prices, rapid response to changing market conditions, and the elimination of emotional decision-making.
- **How It Differs**: The main distinction lies in its automated nature, which allows for trading strategies to be executed with precision and without the need for constant monitoring by the trader.

5.3.2 Risks Associated with Algorithmic Trading

While algorithmic trading can enhance trading efficiency and profitability, it also comes with its own set of risks:

- **Technical Failures**: The reliance on technology means that hardware or software malfunctions can lead to significant losses. This includes connectivity issues, data corruption, or system crashes.
- **Market Anomalies**: Algorithmic models may not always predict or adequately respond to unexpected market events or anomalies, potentially resulting in substantial losses.
- **Over-Optimization**: There's a risk of "curve fitting" where algorithms are overly optimized to past data, making them less effective in real-world market conditions.

5.3.3 Risk Management Techniques for Algo Trading

To mitigate the risks associated with algorithmic trading, traders employ various strategies:

- **Back-testing**: Before deploying an algorithm in live markets, it's crucial to backtest it using historical data. This process helps identify the strategy's effectiveness across different market conditions and avoids over-optimization.
- **Setting Maximum Loss Limits**: Implementing hard stops or maximum daily loss limits can protect against unforeseen market movements or technical glitches. This involves setting automatic stop orders or kill switches that deactivate the algorithm after a certain loss threshold is reached.
- **Monitoring Systems for Abnormal Behaviour**: Continuous monitoring of algorithmic trading systems is essential for identifying and addressing any irregularities quickly. This can be facilitated through real-time alerts and automated system checks that flag unusual activity.

Example of Risk Management in Algorithmic Trading:

Imagine an algorithmic trader named Chris who has developed a new trading model based on historical stock market data. Before deploying this model live, Chris conducts extensive back-testing, which reveals that while the model performs well in upward trending markets, it incurs significant losses during sudden market downturns.

To address this, Chris implements a maximum daily loss limit, ensuring that the trading algorithm is automatically turned off if losses exceed 2% of the account value in a single day. Additionally, Chris sets up a monitoring system that alerts him to any unexpected behaviour, such as a spike in order execution errors or a deviation from expected trading patterns.

By incorporating these risk management techniques, Chris is able to minimize the risks associated with his algorithmic trading strategy, protecting his capital while taking advantage of the efficiency and speed that algorithmic trading offers.

Let's delve into additional hypothetical examples to illustrate risk management strategies in algorithmic trading:

Example 1: Addressing Technical Failures

Scenario: Emma develops an algorithm for forex trading that operates around the clock. Given the 24/5 nature of the forex market, her strategy relies heavily on the continuous operation of her trading system.

- **Risk**: Technical failure, such as a server outage or software crash, could prevent the algorithm from executing trades, potentially missing profitable opportunities or failing to exit losing positions.
- **Risk Management Strategy**: Emma sets up a redundant trading infrastructure with backup servers in different locations. She also subscribes to a cloud-based service that automatically switches to a backup system in case of a hardware failure. Additionally, Emma uses a professional service to monitor her system's health 24/7, ensuring immediate troubleshooting of any technical issues.

Example 2: Mitigating Market Anomalies

Scenario: Liam's algorithmic trading model is based on statistical arbitrage in the equities market, exploiting temporary price inefficiencies between related stocks.

- **Risk**: A sudden market event, like a geopolitical incident, could lead to extreme volatility, making his model's assumptions invalid and exposing him to unexpected losses.
- **Risk Management Strategy**: To protect against this, Liam incorporates a volatility filter into his algorithm. This filter temporarily halts trading if market volatility exceeds a predetermined threshold, resuming only when conditions stabilize. Liam also sets up real-time news and social media sentiment analysis tools to detect potential market-moving events, allowing for manual intervention if necessary.

Example 3: Preventing Over-Optimization

Scenario: Sofia has developed a machine learning-based trading algorithm that uses historical data to predict stock price movements.

- **Risk**: Over-optimization, or "curve fitting," where the algorithm performs exceptionally well on historical data but poorly in live markets due to overfitting to past noise rather than identifying underlying market signals.
- **Risk Management Strategy**: Sofia employs a cross-validation technique in her back-testing process, dividing the data into multiple parts to train and test the model on different data sets. She also regularly updates the algorithm with new data and conducts out-of-sample testing to ensure its predictions remain robust across various market conditions. Sofia sets aside a portion of her capital for paper trading the algorithm in real-time before fully deploying it with her actual capital.

Example 4: Comprehensive Monitoring for Algorithmic Trading

Scenario: Noah runs a high-frequency trading (HFT) operation that relies on executing a large number of orders at very high speeds.

- **Risk**: Anomalies in trading logic or data feeds could result in executing unintended trades, leading to significant exposure or regulatory compliance issues.
- **Risk Management Strategy**: Noah implements a layered monitoring system that includes pre-trade checks for order logic and post-trade analysis for unusual patterns or outlier trades. He also incorporates a "circuit breaker" mechanism that automatically halts trading if the algorithm's activity deviates from expected norms by a significant margin or if the account drawdown exceeds a set limit within a short timeframe.

These examples demonstrate the importance of a comprehensive risk management approach in algorithmic trading, highlighting techniques to address the unique challenges posed by the use of automated trading systems.

Chapter 6: The Psychological Aspects of Trading

Section 6.1 Emotional Biases and How They Affect Trading Decisions

6.1.1 Identifying Emotional Biases

Emotional biases in trading refer to the psychological predispositions that affect decision-making, often leading traders to act irrationally. Understanding these biases is the first step towards managing them effectively.

- **Overconfidence Bias**: This occurs when traders have an unjustified belief in their trading abilities, often leading to excessive risk-taking and neglect of potential warning signs.
- **Fear**: The fear of losing money can cause traders to sell their positions too early, missing out on potential gains, or to avoid trading altogether, which can impede portfolio growth.
- **Greed**: Greed can lead traders to take on too much risk in the hope of high returns, disregard risk management principles, or hold onto winning positions for too long, risking a reversal.
- **Confirmation Bias**: This bias leads traders to seek out information that confirms their existing beliefs or predictions, ignoring contradictory evidence that could lead to more informed decisions.

6.1.2 Impact on Trading Decisions

Each emotional bias can significantly impact trading decisions, often resulting in suboptimal outcomes.

- **Overconfidence Bias Example**: John, an experienced trader, believes strongly in his market prediction skills. This overconfidence leads him to leverage his positions excessively, ignoring signs of market reversal. Eventually, a major market downturn wipes out a significant portion of his portfolio because he failed to apply proper risk management.
- **Fear Example**: Emily, after experiencing a substantial loss, becomes overly cautious. Her fear of further losses causes her to exit trades at the first sign of a downturn, missing the longer-term gains as the market recovers.
- **Greed Example**: Alex, influenced by recent success, starts to ignore his usual risk parameters, aiming for bigger and quicker profits. His greed results in overexposure to a speculative asset, which then crashes, eroding his earlier gains.
- **Confirmation Bias Example**: Sarah, convinced that a particular stock is undervalued and will rebound, selectively focuses on positive news about the company, ignoring a series of earnings warnings. This leads her to hold onto the stock as it continues to decline, significantly impacting her portfolio's performance.

6.1.3 Strategies to Mitigate Biases

Recognizing these biases is crucial, but taking steps to mitigate their impact is vital for successful trading.

- **Journaling**: Keep a trading journal detailing the reasoning behind each trade, including emotional state, to identify patterns over time that may indicate bias.
- **Setting Predefined Rules**: Establish strict trading rules for entry, exit, and risk management to follow, minimizing the room for emotional decision-making.

- **Seeking Contrary Opinions**: Actively seek out information and opinions that challenge your market views to ensure a well-rounded perspective before making decisions.
- **Regular Reviews**: Periodically review your trading performance with a mentor or peer group to gain objective feedback on your decision-making process.

By addressing these emotional biases head-on, traders can cultivate a more disciplined, objective approach to trading, enhancing their ability to make rational decisions even under pressure.

Section 6.2 Techniques to Develop Emotional Discipline and Patience

6.2.1 Building Emotional Discipline

Emotional discipline in trading is the ability to remain calm and execute trades based on logic and strategy rather than impulse or emotion. Developing this discipline is crucial for consistent trading success.

- **Mindfulness and Meditation**: Incorporate mindfulness exercises and meditation into your daily routine. These practices can enhance self-awareness and reduce stress, helping you stay focused and calm, even during market turbulence.
- **Stress Management Techniques**: Regular physical activity, adequate sleep, and relaxation techniques such

as deep breathing exercises can mitigate stress and improve decision-making under pressure.

- **Set Clear Trading Rules**: Establish and adhere to a set of trading rules that dictate when to enter or exit trades, how much risk to take, and what conditions lead to a trade adjustment. This structured approach can help in reducing emotional responses to market movements.

6.2.2 Cultivating Patience in Trading

Patience is the capacity to wait for the right trading opportunity, to hold a winning trade to its optimal conclusion, and to accept that not trading is sometimes the best decision.

- **Develop a Trading Plan**: Having a well-thought-out trading plan that includes specific criteria for trade entry and exit can help in waiting for the right opportunities rather than jumping into poorly considered trades.
- **Practice Delayed Gratification**: Engage in exercises outside of trading that require delayed gratification. This could be as simple as saving up for a purchase instead of buying it on impulse, helping to strengthen the mental muscles needed for patience.
- **Review Historical Trades**: Analyse past trades where patience paid off or where impatience led to a loss. This review can reinforce the value of waiting for the right moment to act.

6.2.3 Case Studies
Case Study 1: The Disciplined Trader

- **Scenario**: Jordan, a day trader, used to make impulsive trades based on intraday price movements, leading to high stress and inconsistent results. After incorporating mindfulness into his daily routine, Jordan found himself better able to resist the urge to trade on impulse, choosing instead to stick to his predefined strategy.

- **Outcome**: Over time, Jordan's trading performance improved significantly, with fewer trades but a higher success rate and lower stress levels.

Case Study 2: The Patient Investor

- **Scenario**: Mia, a retail investor, identified a high-potential tech startup but noticed significant price volatility. Instead of buying in immediately, she waited for a price pullback to her identified entry point, resisting the fear of missing out (FOMO).
- **Outcome**: Mia's patience was rewarded when she was able to enter the position at a more favourable price, leading to substantial gains as the company's value increased over the following months.

These case studies highlight how emotional discipline and patience can lead to better trading outcomes. By adopting techniques to manage stress, setting and following clear rules, and practicing patience, traders can improve their decision-making process, leading to more successful trading results.

I will provide more examples related to this section.

Building on the concepts of emotional discipline and patience in trading, let's explore additional examples demonstrating how these qualities can be cultivated and applied to achieve trading success:

Example 3: The Role of Routine in Building Discipline

Scenario: Alex, a swing trader, struggled with consistency in his trading results due to erratic trading habits and decisions driven by short-term market noise.

Solution: Alex decided to develop a strict daily routine that included reviewing market conditions, analysing potential trades according to his strategy, and setting specific times for trading and review. This routine also included non-trading activities, such as exercise and meditation, to help manage stress.

Outcome: The structured routine helped Alex approach trading with a more disciplined mindset, reducing impulsive decisions based on daily market fluctuations. His trading outcomes became more consistent, and his overall stress levels decreased, making trading a more sustainable activity.

Example 4: Using Visualization Techniques to Enhance Patience

Scenario: Sarah, a forex trader, found herself frequently exiting trades too early out of fear, missing out on significant gains.

Solution: To combat this, Sarah began practicing visualization techniques, where she would spend time each day visualizing holding a trade to her predetermined exit point or letting a trade run its course according to her strategy, even when the market volatility made her anxious.

Outcome: Over time, these visualization exercises helped Sarah develop the patience to stick with her trading plan, improving her ability to capture larger market moves and enhancing her overall profitability.

Example 5: Implementing a "Cooling Off" Period

Scenario: Chris, an options trader, often found himself chasing losses, entering into new trades immediately after a loss in an attempt to quickly recoup his funds, which often led to further losses.

Solution: Chris implemented a "cooling off" period into his trading plan. After any loss exceeding a certain threshold, he would take a mandatory break from trading for at least 24 hours to reassess his strategy and ensure that any new trades were not being made out of emotion.

Outcome: This "cooling off" period allowed Chris to approach trading decisions with a clear mind, significantly reducing impulsive, emotion-driven trades. His overall trading performance improved as he was able to stick more closely to his strategic plan.

Example 6: Peer Support Groups for Emotional Management

Scenario: Emily, who trades equities, noticed that her trading decisions were often influenced by her emotions, especially during periods of high market volatility.

Solution: Emily joined a peer support group for traders where members shared experiences, strategies for managing emotions, and offered support and accountability to each other.

Outcome: Participation in the support group provided Emily with new strategies for emotional control and the reassurance that she was not alone in facing these challenges. This peer encouragement helped her maintain discipline and patience, leading to more reasoned and profitable trading decisions.

These examples underscore the importance of emotional discipline and patience in trading, illustrating practical methods and strategies traders can adopt to manage their emotions effectively and improve their decision-making processes.

-

Section 6.3 The Role of Confidence and How to Build It Responsibly

6.3.1 Understanding the Role of Confidence
Confidence in trading is the belief in one's ability to make decisions that will result in profitable outcomes. It's a crucial component of successful trading, as it empowers traders to execute their strategies without hesitation. However, confidence must be grounded in reality and backed by knowledge and experience to be truly beneficial.

- **Impact on Trading Behaviour**: Adequate confidence facilitates a proactive approach to trading, allowing traders to seize opportunities and manage risks effectively. Conversely, a lack of confidence can lead to indecision, missed opportunities, and an over-reliance on external validation for trading decisions.

6.3.2 Building Confidence the Right Way
Developing genuine confidence involves a combination of education, practical experience, and introspection.

- **Education**: Continuous learning about markets, trading techniques, and financial analysis builds a solid foundation for confident trading decisions. This includes staying updated with market trends, understanding financial instruments, and mastering risk management principles.
- **Practical Experience**: Hands-on experience is invaluable. Start with paper trading or small positions to test strategies without significant risk. Reflect on both successful and unsuccessful trades to understand what works and what doesn't.
- **Learning from Failures**: View losses as learning opportunities rather than setbacks. Analysing why a trade didn't work out as planned can provide insights that contribute to future success and confidence.

6.3.3 Avoiding Overconfidence

While confidence is vital, overconfidence can be detrimental, leading to complacency, risk ignorance, and ultimately, trading losses.

- **Maintain Humility**: Acknowledge that the market is unpredictable and beyond anyone's control. Accept that losses are part of trading and that there is always room for improvement.
- **Set Realistic Goals**: Establish achievable trading goals that reflect your skill level and experience. Unrealistic expectations can feed overconfidence and lead to risky behaviours.
- **Continuous Learning**: The markets are always evolving, and strategies that worked in the past may not work in the future. Stay humble by committing to ongoing education and adapting your strategies as necessary.

- **Peer Review**: Regularly discuss your trading strategies and outcomes with trusted peers or mentors. Constructive feedback can provide a reality check, helping to curb overconfidence.

Example of Building Confidence Responsibly:

Jordan, after experiencing a significant loss due to overconfidence, decides to rebuild his trading approach. He begins by enrolling in advanced trading courses, focusing on risk management and market analysis. He practices with a demo account, applying new strategies without financial risk. Over time, Jordan's demo trading results improve, boosting his confidence.

He returns to live trading with small positions, applying strict risk management rules. Each successful trade reinforces his confidence, not because of the profits but because his decisions were based on sound analysis and risk management. Jordan also joins a trading group, sharing his strategies and learning from others' experiences. This network acts as a sounding board, providing valuable feedback that keeps Jordan's confidence in check, preventing it from crossing into overconfidence.

By building confidence through education, practical experience, and peer feedback, Jordan becomes a more disciplined and successful trader.

Chapter 7: Practical Applications and Strategies

Section 7.1 Real-World Examples of Risk Management in Trading

7.1.1 Successful Risk Management Strategies
Case Study 1: The Commodity Trader

- **Background**: Lisa, a commodity trader, specializes in trading crude oil futures. Aware of the commodity market's volatility, especially due to geopolitical tensions and supply-demand imbalances, Lisa has developed a robust risk management strategy.
- **Strategy**: Before entering any trade, Lisa calculates the potential risk and decides on a stop-loss level to limit losses. She also diversifies her portfolio by trading in a mix of commodities, including precious metals alongside oil, to spread the risk.
- **Outcome**: When crude oil prices plummeted unexpectedly due to an unforeseen global event, Lisa's positions were automatically closed at her pre-set stop-loss levels, significantly minimizing her losses. Her diversified investments in precious metals, which often perform inversely to economic downturns, partially offset the losses in oil.

Case Study 2: The Forex Day Trader

- **Background**: Alex, who trades currency pairs in the forex market, focuses on short-term movements to make profits. Knowing the high leverage in forex can both amplify gains and losses, he adopts a disciplined approach to risk management.

- **Strategy**: Alex uses a combination of technical analysis to set precise entry and exit points and employs risk-reward ratios to ensure potential gains justify the risk. He never risks more than 1% of his capital on a single trade.
- **Outcome**: This approach saved Alex from significant losses during a central bank announcement that led to high volatility. While some trades were stopped out, the losses were contained, and profitable trades later in the day more than made up for the initial losses, thanks to his strict adherence to the 1% rule and his risk-reward criteria.

7.1.2 Key Takeaways

From these case studies, several key insights emerge that can be universally applied to enhance risk management in trading:

- **Pre-Defined Stop-Loss Levels**: Always enter a trade with a clear exit strategy if the market moves against you. This protects your capital from significant drawdowns.
- **Portfolio Diversification**: Spreading investments across different assets can reduce the risk of a single market event wiping out your capital.
- **Risk-Reward Ratios**: Before taking a position, assess whether the potential upside justifies the risk. This helps in making informed trading decisions and managing the trade more effectively.
- **Capital Allocation Rules**: Limiting the amount of capital risked on any single trade can prevent catastrophic losses and ensure longevity in the trading world.

These real-world examples underscore the critical importance of risk management in trading. By implementing strict risk management protocols, traders can navigate through market uncertainties with greater confidence, protecting their capital while seeking profitable opportunities.

I will provide some more examples.

Let's delve into additional examples that underscore the practical application of risk management strategies in various trading scenarios:

Example 3: The Equity Swing Trader

Background: Emma is an equity swing trader who focuses on capturing short- to medium-term gains in stock prices. She is keenly aware of the risks associated with holding positions over several days or weeks, including overnight market risk.

Strategy:

- Emma conducts thorough fundamental and technical analysis to select stocks with strong momentum and clear trend patterns.
- She sets a risk-reward ratio of at least 1:3 for all her trades, meaning for every dollar risked, she aims for three dollars in potential profit.
- Emma uses trailing stop-loss orders to protect profits on positions that move in her favour, automatically adjusting the stop-loss level as the stock price moves.

Outcome:

- When a sudden market correction occurred, many of Emma's positions were already protected by her trailing stop-losses, locking in profits before the downturn could erase them. Her disciplined approach to selecting her trades and managing risk allowed her to weather the market volatility with minimal losses and some secured gains.

Example 4: The Cryptocurrency Trader

Background: Daniel trades cryptocurrencies, a market known for its extreme volatility. He's developed a strategy that allows him to take advantage of the market's rapid price movements while managing the inherent risk.

Strategy:

- Daniel diversifies his trades across multiple cryptocurrencies rather than putting all his capital into a single coin, reducing the impact of any single asset's price drop.
- He sets tight stop-loss orders for each trade to minimize potential losses and uses limit orders to lock in profits at predetermined levels.
- Daniel keeps a close eye on market news and sentiment analysis to gauge potential market-moving events and adjusts his positions accordingly.

Outcome:

- During a sudden crypto market crash, triggered by regulatory news, Daniel's diversified portfolio and tight stop-loss orders minimized his losses. His attentive monitoring of news allowed him to exit positions before the full impact of the crash, demonstrating the importance of staying informed and ready to act.

Example 5: The Options Strategy Trader

Background: Sarah specializes in options trading, using various strategies to hedge her portfolio against market downturns and to generate steady income through premium collection.

Strategy:

- Sarah uses covered calls to generate income on stocks she already owns, selling call options at a higher price than her purchase price to collect the premium with a willingness to sell the stock if it exceeds the strike price.
- She employs protective puts as insurance for her long positions, buying put options to protect against a significant drop in stock prices.
- Sarah carefully selects her strike prices and expiration dates to balance potential income against the risk of market movements.

Outcome:

- Her covered call strategy provided additional income during flat or mildly upward trending markets, while her protective puts limited losses during unexpected market drops. This balanced approach allowed Sarah to maintain a relatively stable portfolio value, highlighting the effective use of options for income and protection.

These examples illustrate the versatility of risk management strategies across different markets and trading styles. By applying tailored risk management techniques, traders can protect their capital, maximize their potential for profit, and navigate the complexities of the financial markets with confidence.

Section 7.2 Analysis of Successful Trades and Lessons Learned

7.2.1 Components of a Successful Trade
Successful Trade Example 1: The Disciplined Entry and Exit

- **Initial Analysis**: Jane identified a strong uptrend in a technology stock through technical analysis, noting a breakout above resistance with increasing volume. She also considered the company's recent earnings beat as a fundamental catalyst.
- **Execution**: Setting a buy order just above the resistance level, Jane predetermined her exit strategy: a target price based on the stock's historical resistance levels and a stop-loss just below the recent support level to minimize potential loss.
- **Post-Trade Review**: The stock hit Jane's target price within two weeks, prompting her to sell and lock in her profits. Reviewing the trade, she noted that her disciplined adherence to her exit strategy was key, as the stock price retraced shortly after.

Lessons Learned:

- **Risk Assessment and Management**: By setting a stop-loss, Jane managed her risk effectively, ensuring that potential losses would not exceed her tolerance level.
- **Importance of Discipline**: Sticking to her predetermined exit plan allowed Jane to realize profits without being swayed by greed or fear.

7.2.2 Lessons Learned
Successful Trade Example 2: Adapting to Market Signals

- **Initial Analysis**: Mike, trading foreign exchange pairs, noticed a divergence between the EUR/USD price action and a leading momentum indicator, suggesting a potential reversal.
- **Execution**: He entered a short position, with a tight stop-loss above the recent high and a profit target at a key support level identified through historical price analysis.
- **Post-Trade Review**: The EUR/USD pair indeed reversed, and Mike hit his profit target. He credited his success to his quick response to the divergence signal and his commitment to the trading plan.

Lessons Learned:

- **Responsive to Market Signals**: Mike's success underscored the value of being observant and responsive to technical indicators that signal market reversals.
- **Objective Decision Making**: By relying on technical analysis and a predefined trading plan, Mike removed emotional bias from his trading decision, focusing instead on objective market signals.

Successful Trade Example 3: Leveraging Economic Events

- **Initial Analysis**: Sarah anticipated increased volatility in the GBP/USD pair ahead of a major Brexit vote. She analysed potential scenarios and their likely impact on the currency pair.
- **Execution**: Based on her analysis, Sarah decided to place a straddle trade, setting up both a call and put option with the same strike price and expiration date, allowing her to profit from the expected volatility without having to predict the direction.
- **Post-Trade Review**: Following the vote, the GBP/USD moved sharply, and Sarah's put option became highly profitable. She managed to close both positions swiftly, capitalizing on the market's reaction to the event.

Lessons Learned:

- **Strategic Use of Options**: Sarah's approach demonstrated how options could be used strategically to benefit from market volatility while managing risk.
- **Preparation and Planning**: Her thorough preparation for the event and understanding of different market scenarios enabled her to devise a trading strategy that was resilient to uncertainty.

These examples illustrate that successful trades often share common elements: thorough initial analysis, disciplined execution, and insightful post-trade review. Each successful trade provides valuable lessons on risk management, the necessity of discipline, and the importance of adapting strategies based on market analysis and economic events.

I will provide more examples for this section

let's delve into additional examples illustrating the analysis of successful trades and the valuable lessons they offer:

Example 4: Capitalizing on Market Corrections

Background: Thomas, a seasoned equity trader, closely monitors market cycles and sentiment indicators to identify potential correction phases in an otherwise bullish market.

Initial Analysis: Observing overextended valuations and bearish divergence in momentum indicators, Thomas predicts a short-term market correction is imminent.

Execution: He strategically positions himself in short-term inverse ETFs that would gain from a market downturn, setting a clear profit target and a tight stop-loss to mitigate risk.

Post-Trade Review: The market experiences a correction as anticipated, and Thomas's positions in inverse ETFs yield substantial profits. He exits his positions upon reaching his profit targets, adhering strictly to his exit strategy.

Lessons Learned:

- **Market Cycle Analysis**: Thomas's success underscores the importance of understanding market cycles and sentiment indicators to anticipate corrections.
- **Risk-Control Measures**: The use of stop-loss orders and profit targets ensured that Thomas could capitalize on the market's movement while managing his exposure to risk effectively.

Example 5: Trading Based on Earnings Announcements

Background: Emily is an adept trader who specializes in trading stocks around their earnings announcements, leveraging the volatility for potential gains.

Initial Analysis: Through fundamental analysis, Emily identifies a company likely to exceed market expectations for its quarterly earnings based on its recent performance and sector trends.

Execution: She buys the stock a few days before the earnings release, setting a profit target based on historical post-earnings movements and a stop-loss to protect her investment.

Post-Trade Review: The company reports better-than-expected earnings, leading to a significant stock price jump. Emily sells her position near the peak of the post-announcement rally, realizing a hefty profit.

Lessons Learned:

- **In-depth Fundamental Analysis**: Emily's ability to pick winners is attributed to her thorough analysis and understanding of company fundamentals and market expectations.
- **Timing and Exit Strategy**: Her trade exemplifies the importance of timing in volatile trading situations and the necessity of having a solid exit strategy to lock in gains.

Example 6: Utilizing Technical Breakouts for Forex Trading

Background: Liam is a forex trader who focuses on identifying and trading breakout patterns, a strategy that allows him to enter trades with a high potential for rapid gains.

Initial Analysis: Monitoring the USD/JPY pair, Liam notices a consolidating triangle pattern forming, indicating a potential breakout.

Execution: Once the price breaks above the triangle's resistance, Liam enters a long position, setting his profit target at the next major resistance level and a stop-loss just below the breakout point to minimize potential losses.

Post-Trade Review: The breakout leads to a strong upward trend, and Liam's position hits the profit target. He reviews the trade, noting the precision of the breakout signal and the effectiveness of his risk management strategy.

Lessons Learned:

- **Technical Pattern Recognition**: This trade highlights the value of recognizing and acting on clear technical patterns in the forex market.
- **Strategic Risk Management**: Liam's careful placement of stop-loss and profit target orders demonstrates a disciplined approach to managing risk and securing profits in a highly volatile environment.

These examples further illustrate that successful trading hinges on a combination of meticulous analysis, disciplined execution, and reflective post-trade reviews. By learning from each trade, traders can refine their strategies, enhance their decision-making processes, and improve their overall trading performance.

Section 7.3 Case Studies of Poor Risk Management and the Lessons from Those Experiences

7.3.1 Analysing Failures
Case Study 1: Ignoring Stop-Loss Orders

- **Background**: Michael, a novice trader, invested in a high-growth tech stock without setting a stop-loss order, believing that the stock's upward trajectory was guaranteed.
- **What Went Wrong**: When unexpected negative news hit the tech sector, the stock's price plummeted. Michael, paralyzed by the sudden downturn, held onto his position, hoping for a rebound that never materialized, leading to significant losses.
- **Missteps in Risk Management**: The critical mistake was Michael's failure to set a stop-loss order, a fundamental risk management tool that could have limited his losses automatically.

Case Study 2: Over-Leverage in Forex Trading

- **Background**: Sarah, attracted by the potential for high returns, used excessive leverage on a currency trade, expecting the market to move in her favour based on a short-term trend analysis.

- **What Went Wrong**: The forex market is notoriously volatile, and an unexpected geopolitical event caused the currency pair to move sharply against Sarah's position. The over-leverage magnified her losses, leading to a margin call.
- **Missteps in Risk Management**: Sarah's primary error was the misuse of leverage, not fully appreciating how it could amplify losses, especially in the highly volatile forex market.

7.3.2 Extracting Lessons

Lesson from Case Study 1: The importance of setting stop-loss orders cannot be overstated. They are essential for automatically closing out a position at a predetermined price, preventing emotional decision-making in the heat of the moment and limiting potential losses.

Strategies to Avoid Similar Mistakes:

- Always set stop-loss orders for all trades, based on your risk tolerance and the volatility of the asset.
- Regularly review and adjust stop-loss levels as necessary to reflect changing market conditions or new information.

Lesson from Case Study 2: The dangers of over-leverage are real and can lead to rapid losses, especially in markets like forex where high volatility is common. Using leverage requires a careful balance and understanding of the potential risks and rewards.

Strategies to Avoid Similar Mistakes:

- Use leverage judiciously, understanding how it works and the potential for magnified losses.
- Conduct thorough market analysis and maintain a well-diversified portfolio to spread risk.
- Implement strict money management rules, deciding on the maximum percentage of capital to risk on any single trade.

General Lesson: Emotional control in trading is crucial. Fear and greed can lead to poor decision-making and risk management failures. Developing a disciplined trading approach, grounded in thorough analysis and a solid risk management strategy, is vital for long-term success.

Strategy for Emotional Control:

- Practice mindfulness and stress reduction techniques to maintain emotional equilibrium.
- Develop and stick to a trading plan, making decisions based on logic and predetermined criteria rather than emotional reactions.

These case studies and lessons underscore the critical importance of risk management in trading. Learning from failures and implementing robust risk management strategies can help traders avoid common pitfalls, protect their capital, and position themselves for long-term success in the markets.

I will provide more case studies of the above.

Case Study 3: Neglecting Market Research

Background: A trader named Alex invested heavily in a commodity based on a tip from a friend, without conducting his own market research or analysis.

What Went Wrong: Shortly after Alex's investment, the commodity's price dropped due to an oversupply issue that was well-documented but overlooked by Alex. His lack of independent research resulted in a significant, avoidable loss.

Missteps in Risk Management: Alex's primary mistake was relying on hearsay instead of conducting thorough market research and analysis, which would have highlighted the oversupply risk.

Lessons Learned:

- **Conduct Thorough Research**: Always perform detailed market research and analysis before entering trades. Depend on reliable sources and data rather than tips or hearsay.
- **Risk Assessment**: Understand the broader market conditions and specific risks to the assets you're trading.

Case Study 4: Failure to Adapt to Market Changes

Background: Emily, a long-term investor in the energy sector, failed to adjust her portfolio in response to clear signs of a shift towards renewable energy sources.

What Went Wrong: As the market increasingly favoured renewable energy over traditional energy sources, Emily's investments in oil and gas companies suffered. Her attachment to her initial analysis and reluctance to adapt led to a prolonged decline in her portfolio's value.

Missteps in Risk Management: Emily's mistake was her failure to adapt her investment strategy in light of changing market trends and conditions.

Lessons Learned:

- **Stay Informed and Flexible**: Keep abreast of industry trends and be willing to adjust your strategy as necessary.
- **Portfolio Reassessment**: Regularly reassess your portfolio to ensure it aligns with current market conditions and future outlooks.

Case Study 5: Excessive Trading Based on Emotion

Background: John, influenced by rapid market movements and the fear of missing out (FOMO), engaged in excessive day trading, constantly buying and selling based on short-term market fluctuations.

What Went Wrong: Caught in a cycle of reactionary trading, John incurred high transaction costs and capital gains taxes, eroding his profits and ultimately resulting in net losses.

Missteps in Risk Management: John's trading was driven by emotion rather than a disciplined strategy. His excessive trading amplified risks and costs, overshadowing potential gains.

Lessons Learned:

- **Discipline and Strategy Over Emotion**: Implement a disciplined trading strategy that focuses on long-term goals rather than reacting to short-term market movements.
- **Understand the Costs**: Be aware of the impact of transaction costs and taxes on trading profitability.

These hypothetical case studies highlight the importance of sound risk management practices, including thorough research, flexibility in strategy, and the need for emotional discipline in trading. By learning from these scenarios, traders can develop strategies to avoid similar pitfalls, focusing instead on informed decision-making and prudent risk management to achieve sustainable success in the markets.

Chapter 8: Building a Growth-Oriented Portfolio

Section 8.1 Strategies for Long-term Wealth Growth through Trading

8.1.1 Growth Investing Strategies
Growth Investing Strategies involve focusing on stocks or assets that exhibit signs of above-average growth compared to their industry or the overall market, even if they may appear overvalued by traditional valuation metrics. These strategies

are particularly effective in emerging markets and technology-driven sectors where innovation and market disruption can lead to rapid growth.

- **Example**: Consider a technology startup that has developed a revolutionary new product. Despite its current lack of profitability, the company's potential to capture a significant market share makes it an attractive growth investment. Traders might analyse the company's revenue growth rate, market penetration strategies, and the overall size of the addressable market to gauge its growth potential.

8.1.2 Diversification for Growth

Diversification is key to managing risk while pursuing growth. By investing across different sectors, geographical regions, and asset classes, traders can reduce the impact of a poor performance in any single investment on their overall portfolio.

- **Example**: Sarah's portfolio includes investments in technology firms, renewable energy companies, and healthcare startups. She also holds positions in emerging markets to capitalize on global growth opportunities. This diversification strategy spreads risk across various sectors and regions, ensuring that a downturn in one area won't derail her long-term wealth growth objectives.

8.1.3 Use of Leverage Wisely

Leverage can be a powerful tool for enhancing returns, but it must be used judiciously to avoid excessive risk. Proper use of leverage involves borrowing money at a lower rate of interest than the expected rate of return on the investment, amplifying potential profits without taking on undue risk.

- **Example**: Mark employs leverage by taking a margin loan to invest in a diversified portfolio of high-growth stocks. He carefully calculates the amount of leverage to ensure it aligns with his risk tolerance and the volatility of his investments. Mark's strategy is to use leverage to enhance his returns but maintains a buffer to accommodate market volatility and avoid margin calls.

Leveraging Compound Interest and Dividends for Wealth Accumulation

One of the most powerful concepts in investing is **compound interest**, where earnings on an investment generate their own earnings over time. Traders focusing on long-term wealth growth pay attention to assets that offer compounding returns, such as stocks that pay dividends which can be reinvested.

- **Example**: Emily invests in a diversified portfolio of dividend-paying stocks. She reinvests the dividends to purchase additional shares, benefiting from both the appreciation of her investments and the compound growth of her dividend earnings. Over time, this strategy significantly accelerates her portfolio's growth, illustrating the power of compounding in building long-term wealth.

These strategies represent fundamental approaches to achieving sustainable, long-term wealth growth through trading. By focusing on growth investing, diversification, prudent use of leverage, and leveraging compound interest and dividends, traders can develop a robust framework for wealth accumulation that balances potential returns with risk management.

Section 8.2 Balancing Risk and Reward in Portfolio Construction

The equilibrium between risk and reward forms the cornerstone of strategic portfolio management, ensuring resilience amidst market fluctuations and fostering opportunities for significant growth. This segment elaborates on the methodologies for risk assessment, judicious asset allocation, and the refinement of the risk-reward ratio to cultivate a robust and profitable portfolio.

8.2.1 Assessing Risk Tolerance

Understanding one's risk tolerance is pivotal in crafting a portfolio that aligns with individual financial goals and comfort levels regarding potential losses. Risk tolerance can vary widely among investors, influenced by factors such as investment horizon, financial objectives, and personal experiences with market downturns.

- **Tools and Methods**: Utilize questionnaires and risk assessment tools offered by financial advisors or online platforms to gauge your risk tolerance. These assessments typically examine your financial situation, investment goals, and emotional response to potential losses, providing a framework for decision-making in portfolio construction.

8.2.2 Asset Allocation

Asset allocation, the process of distributing investments among various asset classes like stocks, bonds, and commodities, is instrumental in risk management. By diversifying investments, traders can mitigate the impact of volatility in any single asset class on the overall portfolio performance.

- **Example of Effective Asset Allocation**: John, aiming for a balanced risk-reward profile, allocates 60% of his portfolio to equities for growth, 30% to bonds for income and stability, and 10% to commodities and alternative investments for diversification and inflation protection. This allocation aligns with his moderate risk tolerance, offering growth potential while buffering against market volatility.

8.2.3 Optimizing the Risk-Reward Ratio

Optimizing the risk-reward ratio involves selecting investments that provide the most favourable balance between the potential risks and returns. This does not mean chasing the highest returns without regard for risk but rather seeking out investments that offer the best return potential for an acceptable level of risk.

- **Techniques for Optimization**:
    - **Risk-Adjusted Returns**: Evaluate investments based on their risk-adjusted returns, such as the Sharpe Ratio, which measures the excess return per unit of risk. This helps in identifying assets that compensate adequately for their risk level.
    - **Scenario Analysis**: Conduct scenario analyses to understand how different investments might perform under various market conditions. This can help in identifying investments that offer resilience in downturns and upside in growth periods.

- **Practical Application**: Emily reviews her portfolio to ensure her investments align with her risk tolerance and long-term goals. She identifies a high-growth stock with a favourable Sharpe Ratio, suggesting it offers good returns relative to its risk. She also runs scenario analyses that show the stock's potential to outperform in market upswings while maintaining relative stability in downturns. Confident in her assessment, Emily adjusts her portfolio to include the stock, enhancing her risk-reward profile.

Balancing risk and reward through careful assessment of risk tolerance, strategic asset allocation, and optimization of the risk-reward ratio is essential for building a portfolio capable of enduring market volatility and capitalizing on growth opportunities. This balanced approach enables traders and investors to navigate the complexities of the financial markets effectively, positioning themselves for sustained wealth growth.

I will provide more examples of the above.

I can outline additional hypothetical scenarios to illustrate the principles of balancing risk and reward in portfolio construction:

Example of Assessing Risk Tolerance

Scenario: Sofia, a 35-year-old software developer, is planning her investment strategy. She has a moderate risk tolerance, aiming for steady growth without exposing her portfolio to excessive volatility.

- **Action**: Sofia completes a comprehensive risk tolerance questionnaire that evaluates her financial goals, investment time horizon, and emotional response to market downturns. The results confirm her moderate risk tolerance, suggesting a balanced mix of equities and fixed-income investments.
- **Implementation**: Based on the assessment, Sofia decides that a 60% allocation to diversified equities (including some high-growth tech stocks and stable blue-chip companies) and 40% to bonds (corporate and government) best suits her risk tolerance and growth objectives.

Example of Asset Allocation

Scenario: Marcus, a retired teacher, seeks to preserve his capital while earning a steady income from his investments. He has a low risk tolerance due to his limited ability to recover from significant losses.

- **Action**: Marcus consults with his financial advisor to develop an asset allocation strategy that minimizes risk and focuses on income generation.
- **Implementation**: They decide on a portfolio allocation of 20% in dividend-paying stocks, 50% in high-quality bonds, 20% in money market funds, and 10% in real estate investment trusts (REITs). This diversified approach aims to protect Marcus's capital while providing regular income.

Example of Optimizing the Risk-Reward Ratio

Scenario: Emma, an entrepreneur, is interested in aggressive growth investments but wants to ensure she's not taking on undue risk relative to the potential return.

- **Action**: Emma uses financial analysis tools to calculate the Sharpe Ratios of potential investments, comparing their expected returns above the risk-free rate to their volatility.
- **Implementation**: After her analysis, Emma selects a mix of emerging market ETFs and technology startups with high Sharpe Ratios, indicating that these investments offer a favourable return for the level of risk assumed. She also decides to hedge her bets by investing in a few defensive stocks in sectors like healthcare and utilities, known for their stability in various market conditions.

These examples underscore the importance of a thoughtful approach to assessing risk tolerance, determining asset allocation, and optimizing the risk-reward ratio. By carefully considering these elements, investors can construct a portfolio that aligns with their financial goals, risk tolerance, and market outlook, setting the stage for long-term wealth growth and stability.

The Sharpe Ratio is a measure used to assess the performance of an investment compared to a risk-free asset, after adjusting for its risk. It is calculated by subtracting the risk-free rate from the return of the investment and then dividing this result by the standard deviation of the investment's returns. This ratio helps investors understand how much excess return they are receiving for the extra volatility that they endure for holding a riskier asset.

Formula:

Sharpe Ratio=Sharpe Ratio=$(Ri - Rf)// \sigma i$

Where:

- Ri = return of investment
- Rf = risk-free rate
- σi = standard deviation of the investment's returns (a measure of risk)

Step-by-Step Example of Using Sharpe Ratio:

Step 1: Identify Investment Return
Imagine you're evaluating an equity mutual fund that has had an average annual return of 8% over the past 5 years.

Step 2: Determine the Risk-Free Rate
The risk-free rate is often represented by the yield on government Treasury bills. Suppose the current yield on a 3-month T-bill is 2%.

Step 3: Calculate the Standard Deviation of the Investment
Through analysis or consulting the fund's performance data, you find that the standard deviation of the mutual fund's annual returns over the past 5 years is 5%.

Step 4: Calculate the Sharpe Ratio
Now, plug the values into the Sharpe Ratio formula:

Sharpe Ratio=$(0.08-0.02)/0.05=0.060/.05=1.2$

Interpretation:

- A Sharpe Ratio of 1.2 indicates that for every unit of risk (as measured by standard deviation), the mutual fund has returned 1.2 units of excess return over the risk-free rate.
- Generally, a Sharpe Ratio greater than 1 is considered good, indicating that the investment returns adequately compensate for the risk taken. A ratio greater than 2 is considered very good, and a ratio greater than 3 is considered excellent.
- In Emma's case, with a Sharpe Ratio of 1.2, the mutual fund offers a favourable return for the level of risk, suggesting it's a worthwhile investment for her aggressive growth portfolio. However, Emma should compare this ratio to those of other investments to ensure she's selecting those with the best risk-adjusted returns.

Practical Use:

- **Comparative Analysis**: Emma can use the Sharpe Ratio to compare the risk-adjusted performance of several investments she's considering. By selecting investments with higher Sharpe Ratios, she aims to construct a portfolio that maximizes returns for a given level of risk.
- **Portfolio Optimization**: By calculating the Sharpe Ratio for her current portfolio and potential new investments, Emma can make informed decisions that could improve her portfolio's overall Sharpe Ratio, thus optimizing her risk-reward balance.

The Sharpe Ratio is a powerful tool for investors aiming to evaluate and enhance their investment strategy, providing a clear metric to gauge the efficiency of generating excess returns for the risk endured.

Section 8.3 Reassessing and Rebalancing the Portfolio

Maintaining a portfolio that aligns with your long-term financial goals and adapts to the evolving market landscape is essential for sustained growth. Regular reassessment and strategic rebalancing ensure that your investment strategy remains effective, optimizing your portfolio's performance over time.

8.3.1 Timing for Reassessment
Guidance on Review Frequency:

- **Annual Review**: At a minimum, conduct a comprehensive portfolio review once a year. This regular check-in allows you to adjust for significant market changes or shifts in your financial objectives.
- **Life Events**: Major life events such as marriage, the birth of a child, a career change, or approaching retirement are critical times to reassess your portfolio to ensure it reflects your current and future financial needs.
- **Market Volatility**: During periods of high market volatility, consider more frequent reviews to adjust your investment strategy in response to rapid changes in market conditions.

8.3.2 Indicators for Rebalancing
Signals That It's Time to Adjust:

- **Asset Allocation Drift**: A significant shift in your asset allocation from your target mix can expose you to higher risk or lower growth potential than desired. For example, if equity markets have performed well, the proportion of stocks in your portfolio may exceed your target allocation, necessitating a rebalance.
- **Changes in Risk Tolerance**: If your risk tolerance has changed due to personal circumstances or closer proximity to retirement, rebalancing to align with your current risk profile is crucial.
- **Underperformance**: Consistent underperformance of certain assets or sectors compared to their benchmarks may prompt a reassessment of their place in your portfolio.

8.3.3 Methods for Effective Rebalancing
Strategies for Efficient Portfolio Adjustment:

- **Tax Considerations**: Be mindful of the tax implications of selling assets. Consider tax-efficient rebalancing strategies such as selling assets in tax-advantaged accounts like IRAs or 401(k)s where possible to minimize capital gains taxes.
- **Transaction Costs**: Evaluate the costs associated with rebalancing, including brokerage fees and bid-ask spreads. Opt for commission-free trades or low-cost brokers to reduce expenses.
- **Rebalancing Bands**: Implement rebalancing bands around your target asset allocations. For example, if your target allocation to stocks is 60%, you might set bands at 55% and 65%. Only rebalance if the allocation drifts outside these bands, minimizing unnecessary trades and maintaining strategic focus.

Step-by-Step Example:

Step 1: **Annual Portfolio Review**

- Alex conducts his annual portfolio review and notices his stock allocation has increased to 70% of his portfolio due to a strong stock market performance, diverging from his target allocation of 60%.

Step 2: **Identify Need for Rebalancing**

- Recognizing this drift as a risk that doesn't align with his moderate risk profile, Alex decides it's time to rebalance.

Step 3: **Consider Tax Implications**

- Alex identifies stocks in his portfolio with substantial gains. To minimize taxes, he decides to sell off some of these stocks in his IRA account where transactions won't incur capital gains taxes.

Step 4: **Execute Rebalancing**

- He sells excess stocks and reallocates the proceeds into bonds and international equities to return to his original asset allocation, carefully executing trades to minimize transaction costs.

By regularly reassessing and rebalancing their portfolio, investors like Alex can ensure their investment strategy remains aligned with their financial goals, risk tolerance, and the changing market conditions, thereby positioning themselves for long-term financial success.

I will Provide more examples:

Example 1: Responding to Economic Downturn

Background: Emma's portfolio is heavily invested in cyclical stocks that perform well during economic expansions. However, leading economic indicators begin to show signs of an impending recession.

Step 1: Market Trend Analysis

- Emma conducts a detailed analysis of current economic indicators, including declining consumer spending and manufacturing output, suggesting the onset of a recessionary period.

Step 2: Reassessment of Portfolio

- Recognizing her current portfolio's vulnerability to economic downturns, she decides it's crucial to reassess her investment strategy to mitigate potential losses.

Step 3: Strategic Rebalancing

- To adjust her portfolio, Emma reduces her exposure to cyclical stocks and reallocates funds to defensive sectors like utilities and consumer staples, which tend to perform better during economic contractions. She also increases her bond holdings to add stability.

Outcome:

- Emma's timely rebalancing before the recession takes full effect helps protect her portfolio from significant losses, showcasing the importance of adapting to changing economic conditions.

Example 2: Shift Towards Sustainable Investments

Background: Jordan is passionate about environmental sustainability and wants his investments to reflect his values without compromising on growth potential.

Step 1: Value Alignment Check

- During his annual portfolio review, Jordan realizes that several of his investments do not align with his commitment to sustainability.

Step 2: Research on Sustainable Investments

- He researches companies and funds with strong environmental, social, and governance (ESG) ratings, identifying those with promising growth potential.

Step 3: Portfolio Rebalancing for Sustainability

- Jordan decides to divest from companies with poor ESG ratings and reallocates his capital to green energy companies and ESG-focused mutual funds, ensuring his investments reflect his values while maintaining growth potential.

Outcome:

- This strategic rebalance not only aligns Jordan's portfolio with his ethical stance but also positions him to benefit from the growing trend of sustainable investing.

Example 3: Preparing for Retirement

Background: Maria is 10 years away from retirement and has a portfolio designed for aggressive growth. As she nears retirement, she wishes to reduce risk and ensure a steady income.

Step 1: Assessing Time Horizon

- Recognizing that her investment time horizon has shortened, Maria evaluates her current portfolio's risk level, deeming it too aggressive for her approaching retirement.

Step 2: Identifying Lower-Risk Investments

- She identifies bonds, dividend-paying stocks, and annuities as lower-risk investments that can provide steady income during retirement.

Step 3: Executing a Gradual Rebalance

- Over the next few years, Maria gradually shifts her portfolio from high-growth stocks to a mix of bonds and dividend-paying stocks, reducing her portfolio's overall risk and volatility.

Outcome:

- By methodically rebalancing her portfolio, Maria transitions to a more conservative investment strategy that secures her financial needs in retirement, demonstrating the importance of adjusting investment strategies based on changing life stages and goals.

These examples underscore the critical nature of ongoing portfolio reassessment and rebalancing in response to personal financial changes, market conditions, and life stages to manage risk and pursue long-term financial objectives effectively.

Chapter 9: Staying Informed and Ahead

Section 9.1 The Importance of Continuous Learning and Staying Informed

The financial markets are dynamic, with new developments occurring at a rapid pace. For retail traders aiming for long-term success, an ongoing commitment to education and staying abreast of market news is not optional—it's indispensable. This section explores the critical role that continuous learning plays in a trader's ability to navigate the complexities of the market effectively.

9.1.1 Adapting to Market Changes

Adapting to Market Volatility: The financial markets are inherently volatile, with prices fluctuating in response to economic reports, geopolitical events, and changes in market sentiment. Continuous learning enables traders to understand the underlying factors driving market movements and to adjust their strategies accordingly.

- **Example**: Consider a retail trader who closely follows and analyses monthly employment reports. By understanding the impact of these reports on market sentiment and monetary policy expectations, the trader can make informed decisions about adjusting their portfolio in anticipation of increased volatility.

Capitalizing on Market Changes: Beyond merely adapting, continuous learning empowers traders to identify and capitalize on new opportunities that arise from market shifts.

- **Example**: A trader who keeps up with developments in the renewable energy sector may recognize early signs of increased investment and government support. By acquiring knowledge about leading companies and technologies in this space, the trader can position themselves to benefit from the sector's growth before it becomes a mainstream investment trend.

9.1.2 Technological Advancements

Staying Updated with Technological Trends: The trading world is increasingly influenced by technology, from algorithmic trading to blockchain and beyond. Staying informed about these technological advancements can provide traders with a competitive edge.

- **Example of Automated Trading Systems**: A trader learns about new software that uses artificial intelligence to analyse market patterns and execute trades based on predefined criteria. By understanding how to leverage such tools, the trader can automate parts of their strategy, potentially enhancing their trading efficiency and effectiveness.
- **Example of Advanced Analysis Tools**: Another trader explores the latest in technical analysis software, which offers sophisticated charting tools, real-time data feeds, and predictive analytics. By incorporating these tools into their trading routine, they can gain deeper insights into market trends and improve their decision-making process.

Navigating Regulatory Updates: The regulatory environment for trading and investing is subject to change. Keeping abreast of new regulations and compliance requirements is essential to avoid potential legal pitfalls and to trade confidently within the framework set by authorities.

- **Example**: A trader stays informed about updates to securities regulations affecting margin trading. By understanding the new requirements, they can adjust their trading activities to remain compliant while exploring the implications of these changes for market dynamics.

Conclusion

The importance of continuous learning in trading cannot be overstated. In a world where market conditions, technological capabilities, and regulatory landscapes are constantly evolving, the successful trader is one who remains committed to education and adaptability. By embracing a mindset of lifelong learning, retail traders can enhance their understanding of the markets, stay ahead of technological trends, and navigate the complexities of trading with informed confidence.

Section 9.2 Resources for Retail Traders

The journey to becoming a proficient retail trader is continuous and requires access to a broad range of resources for education and market insight. This section is dedicated to outlining a comprehensive guide to the wealth of resources available, designed to enhance the knowledge and capabilities of traders at all levels of expertise.

9.2.1 Books and Publications
Books and Publications serve as foundational pillars for understanding the complexities of the market. They offer in-depth insights into various aspects of trading, from the basics of chart reading to the psychological dynamics influencing market participants.

- **"Technical Analysis of the Financial Markets" by John J. Murphy**: A comprehensive guide covering every aspect of technical analysis, essential for traders looking to understand market trends and patterns.
- **"Trading for a Living" by Dr. Alexander Elder**: Focuses on the psychological challenges of trading and offers strategies for managing emotions and developing disciplined trading habits.

- **"The Intelligent Investor" by Benjamin Graham**: Though more focused on long-term investing, this book provides invaluable lessons on market analysis and risk management applicable to trading.

9.2.2 Websites and Online Platforms

Websites and Online Platforms offer timely access to market news, analysis, and expert opinions, crucial for making informed trading decisions.

- **Investing.com**: Offers real-time data, financial news, technical analysis, and a wide array of tools for technical, fundamental, and sentiment analysis.
- **Bloomberg.com**: A leading source for global financial news, providing comprehensive insights into market movements, economic indicators, and company performance.
- **TradingView**: Known for its powerful charting tools and social network where traders share their insights and strategies.

9.2.3 Courses and Certifications

Courses and Certifications provide structured learning pathways, from beginner concepts in trading to advanced strategies and analytical techniques.

- **Coursera & Udemy**: These platforms host a variety of courses on trading, financial markets, and investment strategies, taught by industry experts and university professors.
- **CMT (Chartered Market Technician)** Program: Offers a professional certification for technical analysts, covering a broad spectrum of technical knowledge and ethical practices in trading.

9.2.4 Trading Communities

Trading Communities play a vital role in a trader's development, offering a platform for discussion, experience sharing, and mutual support.

- **Reddit – Subreddits like r/StockMarket and r/Daytrading**: Active communities where traders share insights, strategies, and discuss market trends.
- **Discord Channels**: Various trading-focused servers exist where traders can join live discussions, webinars, and get real-time advice from experienced traders.
- **Forex Factory**: A forum dedicated to forex traders, offering tools like economic calendars, and a platform to discuss strategies and market movements.

Utilizing Resources Effectively

To maximize the benefits of these resources, traders should adopt a proactive learning approach, critically engaging with the material, and applying learned concepts to their trading practice. Diversifying sources of information and continuously updating one's knowledge base are crucial steps in staying relevant and competitive in the fast-paced world of trading.

Moreover, engaging with communities and participating in courses can not only enhance a trader's knowledge but also foster a sense of belonging and support, crucial for navigating the emotional ups and downs of trading. In conclusion, the successful trader never stops learning and leverages a broad spectrum of resources to sharpen their edge in the markets.

Section 9.3 The Future of Retail Trading and Emerging Trends

The landscape of retail trading is continuously evolving, shaped by advances in technology, shifts in regulatory frameworks, and the emergence of new markets and instruments. This section offers a forward-looking perspective on these developments, equipping traders with insights to navigate the future of trading effectively.

9.3.1 Emerging Markets and Instruments

The global financial ecosystem is constantly expanding, introducing traders to new opportunities beyond traditional markets.

- **Cryptocurrencies and Digital Assets**: The rise of blockchain technology has ushered in a new era of digital currencies like Bitcoin and Ethereum, along with an array of tokens and assets that offer novel investment opportunities. The decentralized nature of these assets presents unique market dynamics and volatility patterns, attracting a growing number of retail traders.
- **Fractional Shares**: Platforms now allow traders to buy fractions of a share, making high-priced stocks accessible to investors with limited capital. This democratization of investing enables broader participation in the growth of leading companies.

9.3.2 Technological Innovations

Technology is at the heart of modern trading, driving efficiencies, opening new avenues for analysis, and reshaping the way traders interact with markets.

- **Algorithmic Trading**: The use of algorithms in trading is not new, but advances in computing power and AI are making sophisticated strategies accessible to retail traders. These tools can analyse vast amounts of data to identify trading signals and execute trades at speeds and volumes unattainable by humans.
- **Blockchain for Transparency and Efficiency**: Beyond cryptocurrencies, blockchain technology is being explored for its potential to enhance transparency and reduce transaction costs in trading. Smart contracts and decentralized finance (DeFi) platforms could revolutionize aspects of trade execution and settlement.

9.3.3 Regulatory Trends

As the trading landscape evolves, so too does the regulatory environment. Staying informed about regulatory changes is crucial for compliance and capitalizing on new opportunities.

- **Global Regulatory Divergence**: Regulatory approaches to new trading instruments and technologies vary by jurisdiction. Traders must navigate this complex global landscape to understand how cross-border regulations might impact their strategies.
- **Focus on Consumer Protection**: In response to the rapid growth of retail trading, regulators worldwide are emphasizing consumer protection, transparency, and fair market practices. This could lead to stricter requirements for trading platforms and financial

products, impacting how retail traders access and interact with markets.

Preparing for the Future

To thrive in the evolving world of retail trading, traders should:

- **Stay Informed**: Regularly engage with financial news, industry publications, and regulatory announcements to stay ahead of market trends and changes.
- **Embrace Lifelong Learning**: The continuous evolution of markets and technology necessitates an ongoing commitment to education. Explore courses and resources that cover emerging markets, technologies, and regulatory compliance.
- **Leverage Technology**: Experiment with new trading tools and platforms that leverage AI, blockchain, and other innovations. This not only can improve trading efficiency but also provide insights into market movements and trading opportunities.
- **Engage with the Community**: Participate in trading forums, social media groups, and professional networks to exchange ideas, experiences, and strategies related to emerging trends in trading.

The future of retail trading promises new challenges and opportunities. By understanding and preparing for emerging trends, technologies, and regulatory changes, traders can position themselves to navigate the future landscape successfully and capitalize on the opportunities that lie ahead.

Chapter 10: Creating Your Personal Trading Strategy

Section 10.1 Steps to Develop a Personalized Trading Strategy

A personalized trading strategy is not just a set of rules for buying and selling assets; it's a comprehensive approach tailored to your financial goals, risk tolerance, and the time you can commit to trading. This section provides a step-by-step guide to formulating a strategy that mirrors your unique situation and objectives.

10.1.1 Assessing Your Financial Goals and Risk Tolerance

Start with Self-Assessment: The first step in developing a personalized trading strategy is to conduct a thorough self-assessment. This involves clarifying your financial goals—are you trading for long-term wealth accumulation, supplemental income, or perhaps for the excitement of active trading? Equally important is understanding your risk tolerance. How much of your capital are you willing to risk on individual trades, and what level of market volatility can you comfortably withstand?

- **Example**: If you're a recent college graduate with a stable income and long-term growth aspirations, you might be more inclined to accept higher volatility for the potential of greater returns. Conversely, if you're nearing retirement, preserving capital may be your primary goal, steering you towards a more conservative trading strategy.

10.1.2 Market Analysis Techniques

Introduction to Analysis Techniques: Successful trading strategies are grounded in effective market analysis. This involves both fundamental analysis, which looks at economic indicators, company earnings, and news events to assess asset value, and technical analysis, which uses historical price data and chart patterns to predict future movements.

- **Applying Techniques**: Combining these approaches can provide a more rounded perspective. For instance, fundamental analysis might reveal an undervalued stock with strong growth potential, while technical analysis could help you determine the optimal entry and exit points for trading that stock.

10.1.3 Strategy Selection

Choosing Your Strategy: The trading strategy you select should reflect your trading style and objectives. Day trading, for example, involves making quick trades to capitalize on short-term market movements, requiring a significant time commitment and a high tolerance for risk. Swing trading, by contrast, focuses on capturing gains in a stock within an over-day to several-week timeframe, which might suit those with less time to dedicate daily.

- **Example**: Suppose you have a demanding full-time job but are interested in trading. Swing trading or position trading, which involves holding assets for months or even years, might be more appropriate than day trading, given your available time for market analysis and trading activities.

10.1.4 Setting Up Trade Criteria

Defining Entry and Exit Points: A crucial component of your trading strategy is setting clear criteria for when to enter and exit trades. This might involve specific indicators like moving averages, patterns such as head and shoulders or double tops, or key economic events that could impact asset prices.

- **Example**: You decide to use a combination of the Relative Strength Index (RSI) to gauge market sentiment and moving averages to identify trends. You set a rule to consider buying when the RSI falls below 30 (indicating an oversold condition) and the price is above its 200-day moving average, suggesting an uptrend. Similarly, you might set an exit rule when the RSI exceeds 70 (indicating overbought conditions) or when the price drops below its 50-day moving average, signalling a potential downtrend.

By following these steps—assessing your goals and risk tolerance, mastering market analysis techniques, selecting a strategy that fits your lifestyle, and establishing clear trading criteria—you can develop a personalized trading strategy that positions you to navigate the markets effectively and achieve your trading objectives.

Section 10.2 Incorporating Risk Management into Your Strategy

A robust trading strategy not only focuses on identifying opportunities for profit but also emphasizes protecting investments from undue risk. This section outlines how to weave essential risk management principles into your trading plan to safeguard your capital and enhance your trading longevity.

10.2.1 Establishing Loss Limits

Protecting Your Capital with Defined Limits: One of the cornerstones of risk management is setting clear boundaries on how much you're willing to lose on a trade, over a day, a week, or a month. These loss limits prevent a series of bad trades from significantly depleting your capital.

- **Daily Loss Limit Example**: If your trading capital is $10,000, you might set a daily loss limit of 2%, which equals $200. If you hit this limit, you cease trading for the day, protecting you from further losses and giving you time to assess what went wrong.

10.2.2 Position Sizing and Leverage

Determining How Much to Trade: The size of your positions significantly influences your potential profit and loss. Position sizing should reflect your risk tolerance and the specific trade's risk profile.

- **Position Sizing Example**: Using the 2% rule for a $10,000 account, you wouldn't risk more than $200 on a single trade. If you determine that the stop-loss point for a trade is $1 away from your entry price, you can afford to purchase 200 shares ($200 risk / $1 per share to stop loss).

Responsible Leverage Use: Leverage can amplify your profits but also your losses. It's vital to understand how leverage works and use it judiciously.

- **Leverage Example**: If you use 2:1 leverage on the $10,000 account, you can trade up to $20,000 worth of securities. However, this also means losses are magnified. Ensuring your position size and stop-loss orders account for the increased risk is crucial.

10.2.3 Use of Stop-Loss and Take-Profit Orders

Automating Risk Management: Stop-loss orders can automatically close a position at a predetermined price to limit potential losses. Similarly, take-profit orders can lock in profits by closing a position once it reaches a certain profit level.

- **Stop-Loss Order Example**: If you buy a stock at $50, placing a stop-loss order at $45 limits your loss to $5 per share. If the stock price drops to $45, the stop-loss order is triggered, and the position is closed to prevent further loss.
- **Take-Profit Order Example**: Conversely, if you set a take-profit order at $60 for the same stock, the trade will automatically close once the stock reaches this price, securing your profit without needing to monitor the market constantly.

Implementing Risk Management Practices

Incorporating these risk management tactics into your trading strategy requires discipline and consistency. Regularly review your loss limits and position sizes to ensure they align with your current financial situation and market conditions. Additionally, leverage should be used with caution, always mindful of the amplified risks it introduces.

By diligently applying these risk management principles, you can create a more resilient trading strategy that not only seeks to capitalize on market opportunities but also prioritizes the preservation of capital, setting the stage for long-term trading success.

Section 10.3 Testing and Refining Your Approach

Developing a trading strategy is just the beginning. Before risking real capital, it's crucial to validate and refine your approach. This section outlines practical steps to test your trading strategy, ensuring its effectiveness and adaptability to market conditions.

10.3.1 Back-testing

Validating Your Strategy with Historical Data: Back-testing involves simulating your trading strategy using historical market data to determine how it would have performed in the past. This process helps identify the strategy's strengths and weaknesses and its potential profitability.

- **How to Backtest**:
    1. **Select the Asset and Time Frame**: Choose the market or asset and the historical period over which you wish to test your strategy.
    2. **Apply Your Strategy**: Implement your entry and exit criteria, including any indicators or filters you use to signal trades.
    3. **Analyse the Results**: Evaluate the performance metrics, such as win rate, average return per trade, drawdowns, and overall profitability.
    4. **Adjust and Optimize**: Make necessary adjustments to improve performance or reduce risk based on your analysis.

- **Example**: Suppose you have a strategy that involves buying a stock when its 50-day moving average crosses above its 200-day moving average and selling when the opposite occurs. Back-testing this strategy over several years of data for a particular stock can reveal how often this scenario occurs, the average profit or loss per trade, and the strategy's overall success rate.

10.3.2 Paper Trading

Simulating Trades in Real-Time: Paper trading allows you to trade in real-time market conditions without risking actual money. Many platforms offer paper trading features, providing a realistic trading environment to test strategies.

- **Executing Paper Trades**:
    1. **Set Up a Paper Trading Account**: Choose a platform that offers a realistic simulation of the trading environment.
    2. **Implement Your Strategy**: Make trades based on your strategy's criteria, using the virtual funds in your account.
    3. **Track Performance**: Monitor your trades and portfolio performance just as you would with real trading.
    4. **Iterate**: Use the insights gained to refine your strategy, adjusting your criteria and risk management rules as needed.
- **Example**: If your strategy involves trading forex based on certain economic announcements, you can use paper trading to see how these trades would perform in real-time, adjusting your entry, exit, and position sizing techniques based on the outcomes.

10.3.3 Continuous Learning and Adaptation

Evolving Your Strategy Over Time: The financial markets are dynamic, and a successful trader must be willing to learn continuously and adapt their strategy to changing market conditions.

- **Staying Informed**: Keep abreast of market trends, economic developments, and technological advancements that could impact your trading approach.
- **Regular Review**: Periodically review your trading performance, identifying areas for improvement or adjustment in response to market changes.
- **Adaptation**: Be prepared to modify your strategy, incorporating new techniques or tools to enhance its effectiveness.
- **Example**: After a year of trading, you notice that your strategy performs well in volatile markets but poorly in stable conditions. This insight might lead you to develop separate sets of criteria for different market environments or to adjust your risk management rules to better capture profits and minimize losses.

Conclusion

Testing and refining your trading strategy is a continuous process that plays a crucial role in achieving long-term trading success. By rigorously back-testing, engaging in realistic paper trading, and committing to ongoing learning and adaptation, you can develop a robust trading approach that remains effective in the ever-evolving landscape of the financial markets.

Conclusion of the Book

Summary of Key Points

In this book, we've embarked on a comprehensive journey through the essentials of retail trading, emphasizing the critical role of risk management and the development of robust trading strategies. We started by laying the foundation with an understanding of the financial markets and the various instruments available to traders. We then delved into the fundamentals of risk management, highlighting the importance of position sizing, stop-loss orders, and diversification. Advanced strategies, including leveraging options for risk management and understanding hedging techniques, were explored to provide readers with a toolkit for protecting their investments. The psychological aspects of trading were addressed, recognizing the influence of emotional biases and the importance of discipline and patience. Practical applications and strategies brought real-world insights into successful and unsuccessful trades, offering valuable lessons. Building a growth-oriented portfolio was discussed, with strategies for long-term wealth accumulation. The necessity of staying informed and ahead through continuous learning and adaptation to emerging trends in retail trading was underscored. Finally, we outlined steps to create a personalized trading strategy, integrating risk management, and refining the approach through testing.

Encouragement for the Journey Ahead

As you close this book and embark on your trading journey, remember that the path to success in trading is not linear. It is filled with challenges and learning opportunities. Stay committed to your goals, be patient with your progress, and remain adaptable to the ever-changing market dynamics. The principles and strategies outlined in this book are designed to equip you with the knowledge to navigate these challenges effectively. Embrace continuous learning, leverage the community of traders, and use the tools and resources available to you to stay informed and ahead.

Final Thoughts on the Importance of Risk Management and Continuous Improvement

Risk management is not just a set of rules to follow; it's a mindset that should permeate every aspect of your trading. It's about making informed decisions, protecting your capital, and positioning yourself for sustainable growth. Combine this with a commitment to continuous improvement—regularly evaluating your strategies, learning from your experiences, and staying abreast of new developments in the trading world—and you will build a resilient trading practice. Remember, in the world of trading, the most successful traders are those who not only seek to maximize profits but also understand the importance of protecting against losses. Keep this philosophy at the core of your trading activities, and you will be well on your way to achieving your financial goals.

As you continue on your trading journey, let this book serve as a guide and a reminder of the principles that can lead to success. Trading is as much about personal growth as it is about financial gain. Embrace the journey with an open mind, a dedication to learning, and a commitment to applying the risk management and trading strategies that resonate with your unique situation. Here's to your success in the dynamic and rewarding world of retail trading.

www.ingramcontent.com/pod-product-compliance
Lightning Source LLC
Chambersburg PA
CBHW071046290526
45795CB00004B/1347